CW00742434

Stirring the Fire

Prayers about wishes'
Martyn & Fay

Martyn & Fay Perry

Stirring the Fire

Exploring New Patterns of Ministry

TATE PUBLISHING & Enterprises

Stirring the Fire
Copyright © 2009 by Martyn & Fay Perry. All rights reserved.

No part of this publication may be reproduced, stored in a retrieval system or transmitted in any way by any means, electronic, mechanical, photocopy, recording or otherwise without the prior permission of the author except as provided by USA copyright law.

Scripture quotations marked "NIV" are taken from the Holy Bible, New International Version ®, Copyright © 1973, 1978, 1984 by International Bible Society. Used by permission of Zondervan Publishing House. All rights reserved.

The opinions expressed by the author are not necessarily those of Tate Publishing, LLC.

This book is designed to provide accurate and authoritative information with regard to the subject matter covered. This information is given with the understanding that neither the author nor Tate Publishing, LLC is engaged in rendering legal, professional advice. Since the details of your situation are fact dependent, you should additionally seek the services of a competent professional.

Published by Tate Publishing & Enterprises, LLC
127 E. Trade Center Terrace | Mustang, Oklahoma 73064 USA
1.888.361.9473 | www.tatepublishing.com

Tate Publishing is committed to excellence in the publishing industry. The company reflects the philosophy established by the founders, based on Psalm 68:11,
"The Lord gave the word and great was the company of those who published it."

Book design copyright © 2009 by Tate Publishing, LLC. All rights reserved.
Cover design by Blake Braser
Interior design by Joey Garrett

Published in the United States of America

ISBN: 978-1-61566-446-7
1. Religion / Christian Ministry / General
2. Religion / Christianity / General
09.12.11

To Jamie, Tristan, and Catherine.

Acknowledgments

We're so grateful to our families for all their encouragement over the years; it's good to know that they are always there for us. We'd like to thank all our friends in the clergy support group for sane and wise advice; we've come to rely heavily on their prayer support and their fellowship.

Without the encouragement and support of the Archbishop of Wales none of this story would have been written. We've valued his advice over the years.

Caroline Pascoe has been such a good friend to us and to the parish here. So much that has been achieved in the parish would not have been achieved without her wisdom and guidance!

Everyone at Tate Publishing has continued to amaze us with their kindness, professionalism, and energy. Thank you so much.

A massive thank you too for all in Cilybebyll parish for their faith in God and their willingness to seek his will.

Finally, thanks to God for the way he has met all our needs in life and ministry "according to the riches of his glory in Christ Jesus," (Philippians 4:19, NIV).

Table of Contents

Foreword

"Let us dream of a church ... without the answers but asking the right questions ... unafraid of change, able to recognise God's hands in the revolutions ... a ministering community rather than a community gathered round a minister ... so salty and yeasty that it really would be missed if no longer around ... so deeply rooted in gospel and tradition that, like a living tree, it can swing in the wind and constantly surprise us with new blossoms ... "

—From sermons and addresses by Bishop Wes Frensdorff[1]

In this book Martyn and Fay reflect honestly and movingly on the questions their South Wales parish has asked, the journey of discovery they have shared together, and the new blossoms with which God has surprised them.

Inspirational Ministry Development Bishop Wes Frensdorff dreamt of a church in which "the Spirit is not a party symbol but wind and fire in everyone, gracing the church with a kaleidoscope of gifts and constant renewal of all." This is a story of fire catching through faithfulness to God's call to live and proclaim the gospel, in this generation, in one particular place. It is told thoughtfully and openly, not as a blue-print, but as an encouragement to other churches and parishes, wherever they are, to step out on their own journey of discovery together with God.

The journey described has gone deep into the heart of what it is to be Christian and to be church. Martyn and Fay have grappled with how to lead in ways that will grow confidence, discipleship and commitment. They share here their experience of prayerfully and patiently working to build a collaborative local church culture based on: listening to discern God's call; discovering shared vision to guide action; growing trust, mutual respect and accountability; learning to meet and take decisions in ways that foster openness, participation and collaboration. Through it all they have worshipped together, prayed together, cried and celebrated together, and grown as Christians and churches in their calling to be living signs and agents of God's kingdom.

This is not just a local story: the questions they have asked, the issues they have faced, the encouragements they have seen, are being asked, faced and seen across denominations and internationally today.

It has been a privilege and inspiration to be a companion on this unfolding journey with these faithful people, and I commend their story to you.

—Caroline Pascoe
Ministry Development Officer,
Llandaff Diocese, Church in Wales.
The Feast of The Transfiguration, 2009

About the Authors

We met 30 years ago when our Church youth groups formed a Christian choir to put on evangelistic events. In the early days we staged musicals by Jimmy and Carol Owens. In "The Witness," one of us played Judas Iscariot and the other was part of a group of dancers which condemned him! We continued dating later in college in Cardiff, as "Judas" trained for the Ministry, and the dancer studied to become a podiatrist!

We had the privilege of spending part of our early married life, with two small children, in London, about 160 miles east of the communities in which we had been brought up.

It's surprising how quickly we became used to the crazy pace of life in a big city. On days off from Church work, we'd bundle the children and the double push-chair onto the underground train and head to Covent Garden for croissants and cappuccino for breakfast. Living in the capital it became normal for the children to see people from so many other parts of the world, in London, either as tourists or as those who had moved to England for work or to be near family. On those Saturday mornings in the center of London we would enjoy walks in Hyde Park and time spent in the department stores of Oxford Street. It was so good living in the north of the city, only about 30 minutes away by train from all of the places we'd heard of in earlier life. During these years, we'd visit the Tower of London, the Buckingham Palace, we'd stroll around the museums, and go to the West End to see musicals like Chess, Miss Saigon and Evita. True, a New Yorker once told us that he loved living in London because life was "kinda slow" by comparison with the Big Apple! For us, however, our years in London were a time of frantic busyness and the kind of activity that wouldn't have been possible for us in our home town.

As our time in London drew to a close, it was becoming clear that the next chapters in our life would be written back in South Wales. It isn't always wrong to leave an area where we have been brought up, and it isn't always wrong to move back! God knows the things he has in store for us and listening to him and following where he leads are always the best policy if we want to know his blessing in life. It's when we are in the right place, wherever that is, that we can grow in our life and ministry.

We currently live near Swansea. We have children at University in Cardiff and Nottingham. The Rectory where we live is shared with a hamster called Homer and a cat called Danny. Danny thinks he's rather special and is proof of the old saying "dogs have owners, cats have servants." Danny has his own profile on Facebook!

As we took our daily walks near our home, the idea

for the book started to come together. We made notes under the various chapter headings and kept passing the material back and forth between us as it grew. As the months passed, early drafts were revised and then revised again. The end result comes from both of us. We hope that is not confusing as each chapter contains material from both of us.

Introduction

This book is the story of the changes our parish has encountered over the last eleven years or so in the areas of ministry and decision-making. We are on a journey and certainly haven't arrived. We don't claim to have found all the answers or to have made all the correct choices and decisions. However, we are excited by the things that God has been doing in us individually and as a parish and wanted to share them, for these are difficult and challenging days for so many of us in the Christian church.

This is not a blueprint for success but rather a sharing of thoughts and ideas, many of which have started working for us. Each church is unique, and what works in one place may not work everywhere. Ultimately, God is our best guide; the important thing is to walk day by day with the One who longs to bless and help us. The Apostle Paul reminded the church at Philippi that the One who had begun a good work among them would bring it to completion (1:6); not even St. Paul thought that he had "arrived" (3:12).

We hope that we address the issue of why congregations should want to get involved in stirring the spiritual fire that burns within them. Patterns of ministry are changing and this can often be hard to accept. The truth is that when we allow the Holy Spirit to burn within us, we become increasingly prepared to try new things. It isn't that we get sold on the idea that "new" is good and "old" is bad, so it's out with the old and in with the new. All sorts of chaos has been caused in the life of the Christian church over the centuries by people who thought they knew better than everyone who came before them. God isn't encouraging us to develop an addiction to novelty and an indifference to everything we're already doing that works well.

In Luke's Gospel (24:13–35) two believers found themselves walking with the risen Jesus. The Scriptures took on a new meaning as their hearts started to burn within them through their increasing openness to God. They realized that the One who broke the Bread for them was Jesus himself, and they set out for Jerusalem to find fellowship with the other disciples. Before long, the fire of the Holy Spirit stirred them up at the Feast of Pentecost.

When that happened, the young church became willing to live as the Lord directed. Had that not been the case, the Gospel wouldn't have spread to Europe. Centuries later, it wouldn't have crossed the Atlantic and made its huge impact on the newly born United States of America, burning the truth of the Gospel into the hearts of the Founding Fathers. When we open our hearts to God and allow the Spirit to stir up the spiritual fire he brings, we become equal to any challenge and can face the future with real confidence in God. That's the case for us as individuals, families, churches and nations. Quenching the Spirit has the opposite effect!

There is an ancient prayer that is still prayed by many Christians 5 weeks before Christmas day. The prayer became so well known and loved that this day is still known as "stir up Sunday" and the tradition of making and stirring the Christmas pudding on that day still remains! *"Stir up, O Lord, the wills of your faithful people that they might bring forth the fruit of good works"*

Eleven years ago, we arrived in a small, fairly traditional Anglican parish in South Wales. We found lovely people in the mostly elderly congregation, many of whom were deeply committed to God; they had an obvious faith in him. Much of the running of the parish fell on the shoulders of wardens, the lay reader, the minister, and a few others. As tends to be the case in many parishes, one style of worship was on offer.

Today, we have about forty people actively involved in running the parish, five worship styles are celebrated, and the average age is gradually getting younger.

We still have a long way to go but would like to share with you our journey up to now. Over the years, God has been gracious to us in so many ways. It is our prayer that we might all continue to know this in the future.

Pay More, Do More, Get Less?

Pay more, do more, get less? This doesn't seem like a very promising advertising strap line for a company as it attempts to turn a struggling business around. At first glance, this seems to be precisely what we're being told as church members these days.

As Christians, we're well aware that these are challenging times. The church no longer has the place in the community that it once had. Trying to connect with wider society about Jesus has obviously become more difficult now that fewer and fewer people have a working knowledge of the Bible and the words that the church naturally uses. More and more people seem instead to turn to the "mind, body, spirit" sections of our bookshops. If they are aware that they have real questions in life, they seem to be assuming that the answers are not Christian ones.

Added to this, we are aware that a considerable financial crisis has hit the church in recent years. The financial buffeting that people have experienced in wider society hasn't passed the church by. In the light of this, we know that something needs to be done in church life. Far-reaching decisions need to be made, for the church's wealth, accumulated over the centuries, has been affected, as has the centuries-old assumption that there can be a priest in all of our cities, towns, and villages. The problem is that, for so many of us, talk of new patterns of ministry feels like an attempt by the hierarchy to encourage the laity to come to terms with larger, grouped churches and fewer clergy to run them. The answer? In part, the answer to this problem must obviously include the ministry of all God's people. In reality, in the pew, however, it can easily feel like all God's people are being asked to pay ever-rising costs, to do more and more of the work that any half-decent clergyman used to do, and to get less of the kind of ministry that will have given comfort in years gone by. If congregations are to do more, what does this say about the work rate of the minister? It might not be spoken out loud, but the question seems like a good one. "So what's the minister doing these days, a PhD in *CSI Miami*?"

This might indeed feel like how things are for many of us. This feeling might be familiar to many of us; it might also feel like "bad news," but the God of the Bible seems to be very good at bringing great things out of challenging, and even frightening, situations. Toward the end of the lengthy and very beautiful story in Genesis, Joseph is recorded telling his brothers that they no doubt intended bad things for him when they engineered his forced removal to Egypt, "but God intended it for good to accomplish what is now being done, the saving of many lives" (chapter 50: 20, NIV). What is happening in these turbulent times throughout the church might bring to the surface the good practice that God wants us to recover. We might have been comforted by a particular model of ministry in the past; yet, in reality, it has robbed so much of the body of Christ of its opportunity to serve, to minister, and to grow in our faith and maturity in Christ as we pray, study, and work together.

These challenging times might well be God's appropriate time for re-establishing a healthy pattern of church life and ministry. It might be in times like these that we can recapture the breadth of ministry, education, and worship that we might not have embraced had old certainties and old ways been able to continue. Throughout history, God has been involved in his church, gently or sometimes firmly steering her back onto the correct path. Perhaps he is using the current crisis to steer us onto a better path.

Visiting different churches over the years, the holidaymaker, or writer of "The Good Church Guide," might have encountered massive diversity theologically and in terms of preferred worship style, as he or she will have traveled throughout the country. In each community, however, this diversity will have been well and truly hidden. Most churches will largely have celebrated one, single in-house style, depending on whether it was High Church, Low Church, conservative, or liberal. In effect, as congregation sizes collapsed, people will have been "un-churched" if they had longed to see something they needed but wasn't practiced locally. Some people might be helped by frequent communion services, but find that their local church provides something very different. Others might really flourish in a church with an emphasis on Bible teaching and find that the church in their neighborhood only offers sermons that don't exceed ten minutes in length! Perhaps we need to rethink how diverse each community now needs to be. Reconnecting with people for the sake of the good news will have been practically impossible when those outside the life of the church community were told, in effect, "You really are welcome, but this is how we do things here; it's this or nothing."

It might be now, as the ship of the church sails through these choppy waters, that God is asking us whether we are prepared to practice something that is more diverse and genuinely welcoming. Culturally, there is huge diversity in each church, each family, and many of us as couples. We are a case in point. In terms of music preference, one of us, a "head banger" in earlier life, remains a devotee of Meatloaf; the other is an avid listener to the jazz fusion band Weather Report. Deciding which CD to play in the car is an interesting discussion, and yet we continue to be a couple who are enriched rather than undermined by our diversity. When some of us in the pew might love opera and not care much for hip hop, why do we accept a situation where there is simply one worship style on offer amongst us both musically and liturgically? As in the human family, we don't cease to exist as family if we have different tastes. So, in the church family, "different" isn't a problem to solve but part of the masterpiece God wants to create among us.

If new structures are needed to meet the challenges of worship, they certainly are when it comes to the kind of things the Apostle Paul wanted to say about our ministries in the body of Christ. With love as the guiding principle (1 Corinthians 13), 1 Corinthians 12 and 14 have so much to say about our gifts, abilities, and ministries—one body, many parts indeed!

The model of ministry we've received as Anglicans/Episcopalians has seemed to imply that the minister will have all gifts in every area. He or she will be a perfect pastoral visitor. They will be an inspired youth and children's worker, their preaching will be a delight and joy to all who listen (but not too long please; we are Anglican/Episcopalian!), they will lead meetings with grace and managerial skill, settle disputes about flower rotas with the wisdom of Solomon, never get cross or tired even when the phone rings ten times during their meal. This paragon of perfection will always be at home to receive visitors or phone calls while simultaneously always being out visiting the sick and needy! Mission will flow from every pastoral pore. Every detail of mending church roofs and graveyard upkeep will be written upon the clerical brow. In films, the minister even manages to live inside their church whenever detectives wish to call!

In reality, of course, the minister will have many gifts (one hopes) but cannot possibly be an expert in every area or indeed claim to have a deep passion and skill in every area. If we look around our pews, however, we find people with many different gifts, skills, and passions. Paul talks of the church as a body, and God, therefore, will not give us a body with skills missing. God has provided us with the whole body, but for so long we have been content to keep many people sitting motionless in pews. Some of us even have unspoken rules such as: you need to be regularly attending church for at least five years before you are given the honor of joining the church council.

Perhaps God is using the current crisis in church life to remind us of a basic truth: together, we, the people of God, are "church," and we all need to play our part to make sure that God's church is firing on all cylinders. "Church" is not a building I go to once a week while it falls to the minister and a few trusted insiders to run the show. Rather, we, the church, are a group of diverse, talented, God-called individuals who each have things to offer. We each have God-given gifts to use. We each have our part to play in building up others and then reaching out to the wider community in natural and spontaneous mission.

In today's society, we can find it easy to be very critical of others. In some ways, our experience of life can be "dog eat dog." The culture in which we live can easily rubbish people who are "the weakest link," with so much popular TV being based on voting others off or putting others down. So many people feel they are failures, as they do not have the "perfect" body, home, family, job, etc, which our society would have us believe are necessary if we are to live happy and fulfilled lives. Many people carry these assumptions into their church life and believe, as a result, that they have nothing to offer. Yet ours is the God of grace who assures us that he has gifted each of us so that we all have something to give as part of the body of Christ. The parable of the talents in Matthew 25:15 tells us that God has gifted us all "according to his ability," and as we use these gifts for God, they grow, and we grow too.

Do we choose to believe God or the assumptions of the society in which we live? Perhaps God has made it possible for us to be far more involved in the life of our churches than we had ever thought possible. Becoming

more involved in church life might be God's recommended path for us if we are to reach the spiritual and
personal maturity that Christ has earmarked for us
(Ephesians 4:13).

Raising the Spiritual Temperature

All of us as Christians, of course, have a very deep faith in Christ and real experience of God. We have to admit, however, that for some strange reason, some of us are not very good either at talking openly about this reality or about our faith. Perhaps in part this is something to do with certain cultures among us, especially in respect of churches that have tended to be neither evangelical nor charismatic over the years. The experience of God day by day is certainly present for so many of our people, but the culture in which we live tends not to invite us to speak about it in normal conversation.

If we won the lottery or a fortnight's cruise, we would be likely to share the news with anyone who would listen. We'd also do it in a natural tone of voice. Yet, as Christians, although we have a prize above all prizes in Jesus, we often fail to talk naturally about it. Often, we keep church talk strictly for a Sunday for fear of what others might think. How can God's mission be effective in us and through us if we don't know how to talk openly about the most important thing in our lives?

The spiritual temperature would need to be raised in the parish in order to achieve the things we needed to achieve. Talking openly and honestly about our faith and our experience of God would have to become our culture; all of this would have to be normal and natural. If it were not, everything we were trying to put in place would certainly have been doomed from the start; our attempts to change things any other way would have been self-defeating. Nothing attractive or helpful could have been achieved here if the end result looked like a school for the spiritually odd or morally superior.

We are right to argue that spiritual experience is a journey, a pilgrimage. As Anglicans/Episcopalians, we emphasize that coming to know God doesn't always have to be a sudden, one-off experience in order to be real or valid. For some, of course, there is clearly and wonderfully a sudden, definable moment when they go from not knowing God to knowing him. They can remember the occasion of this sudden conversion; St Paul's type of experience clearly still happens today. But for many of us, we grew up in Christian homes and can't really recall a moment when we didn't know and love God. Our spiritual experience was as natural as breathing; it is natural for us to think more in terms of our spirituality growing gradually—our pilgrimage will only be complete when we arrive in heaven. The important thing is to know Jesus for ourselves, as Lord, Savior, and friend; whether we came to know him suddenly or more gradually is less important.

However we have gained our spiritual experience, for each of us, it is important that we move closer to God on a daily basis. The ancient church prayer, "Come, Holy Spirit," needs to be ours day by day, even moment by moment. There are decisions to be made if this is to become a reality, because spiritual growth tends not to develop in a healthy way just by accident. We make decisions in other areas of life and take this to be quite normal if good things are to happen. As Christians, we need to meet with our brothers and sisters in Christ in order to go on learning about our faith, sharing fellowship, and growing in confidence as we practice Christian life and ministry together.

The old chestnut, "I don't need to go to church to be a Christian," tends not to work very well in practice, and it isn't confirmed by the kind of thing we find in the Bible. You certainly don't need to go to church to be a good and helpful person! That much is true. Also, you don't cease to be a Christian if you become housebound; God's grace continues to help us in such circumstances. That's a very different thing from choosing not to be involved in the life of the people of God. A healthy spirituality in the church can be seen as a positive, spiritual fire and ourselves as individual coals. How quickly we cease to glow if we intentionally remove ourselves from the fire. It is only with others that we can feel the positive effect of the fire of the holy love of God.

When we arrived in the parish about eleven years ago, we started by encouraging people to express their real experience of God in word and action. From the start, we tried to encourage parishioners to grow in their experience of God; all of us would need to grow in our faith. God is so gracious to us and is delighted when we, his children, continue to take further, tottering steps toward him.

One way we can encourage people to talk more openly about their faith is to model it ourselves! It was crucial for us in Christian leadership to make clear that we have always talked about our experience of God. This would cut across the view that clergy and their families talk about God because it's their job. They're paid to! It is a widely held theory that people go into theological college "normal" (i.e. not talking about God). Presumably, at some point in the course, they have the operation that turns them into professional Christian and spouse, and their conversation is never quite the same again! We tried to bring God naturally into our conversations from the beginning of our time here. In our conversation, God would have to be shown to be a normal part of everyday life (which he is, of course). When people spoke to us at the end of a service about a difficulty or illness and asked us to pray about something, for example, we would sit with them in a pew at the back of church there and then and quietly pray together. This became a normal part of our church practice.

In addition to this, once a month, both at Sunday and midweek service, people were invited to receive prayer for healing and anointing with oil. This would happen if they chose to stay at the altar rail after receiving communion and hold out their hands. This approach to prayer was simple and short, yet we have seen people's lives changed by it as God met with them and deepened their spiritual experience. We often tend to think of healing purely in terms of physical afflictions, but we needed to learn that emotional and spiritual concerns could be helped by God through prayer as we opened ourselves up to the healing grace of Christ. At our informal services, people could ask to be prayed with for specific things and might result in prayer that would take a little longer.

Teaching the Christian faith in the parish has also been very central and important in raising the spiritual temperature. The Old Testament has taken its place alongside the New in preaching and teaching. Biblical books Jesus used as authoritative were, therefore, taught and taken very seriously here. They weren't binned or sidelined, as this could easily give a distorted picture of God—grace and love are not Christian inventions after all! We believe that God is faithful and doesn't change; the God of the Old Testament is the same One we meet in the New Testament, for in Jeremiah 31:31, the covenant with God in which we share is described as a new covenant with the house of Israel and the house of Judah. How could we possibly understand the New Testament without the Old? The underlying message in all of this will have been about the faithfulness of God; God doesn't call us and use us and then reject us and move on to others. We could all grow in our faith, because God was trustworthy.

Preaching and teaching would also need a practical edge. It would be important to try to work out what the Scriptures might mean for our daily lives in a world like ours. Three times a month, we met for Bible study and discussion. Sometimes this would be as a large group, sometimes as smaller ones in home groups (or cell groups). Daily Bible reading notes have also been made available at both churches. This has been crucial in the raising of the spiritual temperature in the church; people were encouraged to see this spiritual warming of the heart (Luke 24:32) as a natural part of our Christian lives. It was for this reason that we were all encouraged to spend some time each day with God in study and prayer. We produced and gave out a simple order of daily prayer for those who find a more structured type of prayer helpful. This booklet would give some kind of liturgical content to our prayer life. It could be used with the Bible to take away the sense that to develop our spirituality is to "fly solo."

When we started the Alpha course here, we first encouraged church members to attend. The process of "process evangelism" would need to begin with all God's people renewing their faith in Christ and starting to talk about it.

Parishioners also lead a prayer group that meets every fortnight, with the emphasis being on silent prayer and listening to God. This is something we can all do. This has proved to be significant, and, at times, pictures and possible words from God are shared at the end of the session. At root, it seems sensible to treat Christian spirituality as normal and natural. To act as if spiritual experience is for a few "special" ones certainly can create a very narrow and dangerously exclusive church.

In these challenging times for the Christian church, why would people want to pay more, do more, and get less? As our faith in God builds and our love for him deepens, it becomes natural to want to serve. We start to explore the many gifts God has given us. As we do, it becomes a delight to practice our ministries and to encourage others to do the same. We begin to view everything we have and are with the insights of

Christian stewardship. As we grow nearer to the One who gives himself to us completely, we start to want to respond to his love by giving our time, money and gifts in response. To recognize that God wants to use us all is gain in every sense. We do indeed get less of the previous pattern that kept us passive, but that can hardly be a bad thing. The old pattern of paid professionals and passive consumers slowly begins to give way to something that is much more in harmony with the Scriptures. God has done so much for us; we will all need to play our part in praising the Lord (Psalm 150).

Keep the Home Fires Burning

It is so important to be part of a spiritually warm, caring, Jesus-centered church. However, we all have a responsibility to attend to our personal devotional life too. Spiritually warm churches can only come into existence if its individuals and families have an up to date spirituality. The truth is that we all seem to leak like sieves spiritually. We can fill up and have any number of memorable times when God renews and fills us with his love but quickly find we can't simply live on the blessings of the past; we need to go on being filled with the Holy Spirit each and every day. This is true for all of us, and it is doubly true for any who are involved in Christian leadership. How can we encourage others to grow in faith if we are "running on empty?"

Life is busy. We all know that. It would obviously be wrong to imply that only the clergy and those married to them know what busyness is while everyone else in the church wonders what to do with their time.

However, when we live in a clergy home, this does mean that we are living over the shop. At the end of the day, we can't leave work and go home. This can be particularly demanding because we can end up feeling that we are on duty all day, every day—and that includes the day off too. It is not unknown to end up feeling that we only truly "switch off" when the aircraft wheels leave the tarmac and we are heading abroad. These are, of course, important times. How much we have come to value finding good coffee breaks around the Rialto Bridge in Venice and wandering by the sea at Costa Teguise in Lanzarote! Martyn also gets withdrawal symptoms without his annual visit to Jerusalem. Closer to home, we often meet friends in our local Starbucks who, like us, are getting away from a ringing telephone on the day off. How difficult it can be when we live with the reality of never truly being off duty at home.

When life is like this, it is so easy to end up stressed out or having waved good-bye to our spirituality some-time over the years of frantic busyness. There are obvi-ous dangers for all concerned when spiritual experience ends up in a siding like this. Sometimes, we only know that the wheels are coming off our relationship with God when this has been going on for very many years and there is much damage to repair.

The crucial thing is that the coals remain in the fire. Christian leaders, first and foremost, have to be Christians with a living faith and an up-to-date spiri-tual experience. It's against this background that min-istry has to take place for us as clergy and those who are married to them. If this is to be a reality, decisions have to be taken to ensure that our spiritual life remains healthy; it certainly doesn't happen by accident, espe-cially if we end up thinking that self-neglect is part of God's work.

During the second part of 1995, when Martyn

started to reconnect with a healthier spiritual experience following a near miss with burnout, we did indeed start to make those decisions. What would have happened without a renewed resolve to continue to walk with God and recommitment to put him first is anyone's guess. We had encountered so many helpful spiritual practices over the years, but good practice is about us and the decisions we make. When it comes to life and ministry, sanity and spiritual health involve saying yes to some things and no to others; everything can't always be done. Trying to do the impossible should ring alarm bells for us. Over the years, we had both come to a point of cherishing a wide variety of spiritual experiences and practices: the importance of Scripture and the teaching of the faith, the place of liturgy when God's people meet together for worship, charismatic approaches to praise and the use of the gifts of the Spirit. All of these had been picked up over the years and had rightly become so important.

Each of us has found that different things have worked over the years to help our devotional life and spiritual experience remain up to date. As a couple, one of us is certainly a morning bird and prays for two hours before breakfast. The other is more of a night owl, and prefers spending time with God later in the day; morning devotions, if attempted, would soon degenerate into a less than positive version of groans and sighs that are too deep for words. No single pattern is right, with everything else being wrong or fundamentally unspiritual and displeasing to God. However, staggering down to the espresso machine in the morning to find one's partner full of the joy of the Lord can seem to be something of a mixed blessing at times.

Fay had been brought up in the Church in Wales and had also deepened her faith with friends in a local Baptist church and its "Christian Endeavour" group. Martyn had benefited hugely from a Baptist upbringing and will have gained a real sense of the importance of preaching from his pastor. Martyn found that exposure to Anglican/Episcopalian liturgy was positive, helpful, and filled with Scripture. We married in 1986, shortly after which Martyn was ordained a Baptist minister. In the late 1980s, Martyn was received into the Church of England in London diocese, this, gave Fay a sense of "coming back home" to Anglicanism/Epicopalianism.

A year at the College of the Resurrection, Mirfield, followed. It would be difficult to exaggerate how invigorating it was to explore the sacramental and liturgical emphases of the college. The spirituality of the Community of the Resurrection was so wonderful, not least in the way we were able to benefit from worshipping with the community and using a more monastic, community-based approach to daily prayer.

The truth is, however, that even the richest and most helpful of spiritualities can grow cold if care isn't taken to remain aglow in the Spirit during the years of ordained ministry. So often, the enjoyable spiritual hothouse of college can give way to something less invigorating day by day, as prayer, study, and the devotional side of things gradually come off second best to the seemingly unending stream of urgent calls upon our time when there is a parish to run. How good it is that the Anglican/Episcopalian system insists on its clergy saying morning and evening prayer. However, that can easily be rattled off quickly at times instead of spending time delighting in God's presence. Over the years, we discover, to our cost, that spiritual shortcuts don't work.

It will only have been as spiritual practice was being renewed for us that we reconnected with active involvement in charismatic renewal in our diocese. The monthly clergy and spouse support group proved to be something of a spiritual lifeline. How much we came to benefit from the spiritual warmth and obvious sanity of colleagues in renewal. The Celtic insight of seeing everything, even the ordinary and mundane, in the light of the presence of God gained ground for us and helped enormously. As there had been a growing cold—as a result of embracing bad practice—so there was a warming again of the spiritual temperature by God's grace. A daily devotional life was then re-established. Even car journeys provided an opportunity to enjoy God's presence with worship CDs—alongside Meatloaf and Weather Report, of course.

We walk two miles a day, blessed by many beautiful country footpaths near our home. Partly, this is to help our health as middle age catches up with us; partly, it's a chance to wonder at God's creation as we spot a wide range of scenery, birds, and animals, including buzzards, herons, red kites, ferrets, and squirrels. How can you not stop in amazement at God's creation on spying these things and give praise to our Creator? We also use this time to pray for the parish and any other needs we are aware of; the sheep don't seem to mind when we pray out loud.

For us, it has become good to spend time away with God, whether this is a retreat back at Mirfield with the Community of the Resurrection or a week at Spring Harvest. We have come to value these times when we can relax and enjoy God's presence and pause long enough to listen to him. Even on "ordinary" holidays, there will have been times when we will have benefited from going into churches for a few moments with God or enjoying his peace on a balcony somewhere, basking in his presence as we unwound and relaxed.

Part of a healthy practice has also involved ring fencing our day off. Too many clergy seem to boast that they don't have time for a day off. How unwise this widespread example of spiritual self-harm is. It is too easy to burn out and far better to take quality time off and return, refreshed, to the busyness. How important too to spend time together as a couple rather than just waving as you pass, never moving beyond the leaving of notes to each other on the fridge. So, we are always up and out early on the day off and enjoy time together in coffee shops, wandering and then enjoying lunch together.

Before moving on from these few thoughts about spiritual life in the rectory, Martyn also prays monthly with two other colleagues (a group they call "prayer triplets"). This has been crucial for him over the years, in the respect of friendship and fellowship, as they chat first over coffee and share ideas and problems. Time spent together in prayer rounds off these times with others who know some of the joys and trials that ordained life and ministry can bring.

About three years into our ministry in this parish, Martyn went to a four-day retreat for church leaders near Cardiff run by New Wine, a charismatic network. This became crucial for him and for the parish on so many levels. Certainly, as we started to take steps forward as a parish, churchwardens here would later observe how important this week was for all of us.

What Makes a Healthy Church?

Martyn came back from the New Wine Network Leaders' Retreat excited by what he had heard there. As part of the retreat, one of the speakers mentioned a number of characteristics that often tend to be present in healthy churches. This was very different from the things that used to be argued by those committed to church growth. Earlier, the emphasis of teaching days on church growth seemed to be "Do these things if you want to grow." If they had been tried and growth hadn't followed, then they hadn't been tried properly! The end result would be worse than the first, for now guilt would accompany the disappointment that came with dashed expectations of growth.

It seemed to us that the blueprint-type model couldn't possibly be appropriate if a church had a commitment to working with all sorts of different types of people in many different areas. How can one pattern of church life and ministry work for everyone everywhere? Surely, there can't be a single model or pattern that would be guaranteed to work automatically everywhere. Churches are different; clergy and people often are massively diverse. Furthermore, the "do this and grow" model fails to recognize that God leads and directs in different ways, depending on what would be appropriate in different areas. By contrast, the things that were being spoken about at this New Wine leaders' retreat were much more convincing and helpful than that.

Instead, what was being spoken about here was the fruit of observation of the kind of qualities that tend to be present when churches are good and healthful places to belong. Good practice, it was suggested, was more important in itself than us putting in a theoretical approach and asking God to be happy to bless it. When good practice was established, however, growth did often flow from it. The emphasis was more a case of "Be this, and growth will often take care of itself."

The qualities listed were:

- a leadership that empowers others
- ministry of all the baptized in the light of the gifts of the Spirit
- inspiring and diverse worship
- a warm, Jesus-centered spirituality
- loving relationships
- the importance of small groups in the life of the church
- evangelization that meets people at their point of need
- the importance of useful structures in the life of the parish

In many ways, this would be quite a departure for us in the parish if we took these observations seriously in practice, even though they seemed right in principle. We looked at each of these in turn in the meetings of our church council.

Often, in years gone by, the style of ministry practiced by so many church leaders (leaders who were often good and conscientious, it must be said) seemed to be based on a view that held that the cleric was the only real embodiment of leadership and ministry within the church. It would, therefore, be right and proper that the clergy would end up doing the vast majority of the work that needed to be done. What every parish needed was a good, spiritual, and, ultimately, busy church leader. The baptized did not, therefore, need to minister beyond tasks such as cleaning, providing music for the liturgy, and arranging flowers. Whatever its strengths, this approach to ministry and leadership tended not to empower others in the life of the church.

What about the gifts of the Spirit? These, it was suggested, often tended to be present in churches as they grew. For so many of us, the gifts of the Spirit have often been taken to be something of a hot potato in the smooth running of a church. For many, they have been seen as a bit weird, perhaps something of a threat to good and orderly ministry. Throughout the early church, many of the massively diverse believers practiced what we'd call the gifts of the Spirit. In these parts of the church, it was believed that God gave specific guidance in actual situations. What we read in Scripture is advice about their wise use. The gifts of the Spirit weren't to be stamped out but rather used wisely.

Specific advice given by the Holy Spirit in this way would agree with the biblical teachings of the church. Sometimes this might be given through dreams, sometimes through hunches and the overwhelming impressions particular believers had. In 1 Corinthians chapters 12 and 14, Paul gave advice on how these gifts should be used.

Almost certainly, if we have been Christians for a number of years, we'll have had experience of this kind of thing. Perhaps we've known that someone was sad, even though they said they were "fine." There might have been times when we have called in to see someone, even though this had not been our original intention, and this visit made all the difference to the person concerned. Furthermore, not all of our dreams will have been just a random and meaningless processing of events and issues that had been on our minds before we slept. There will always be a practical and beneficial result when we allow the Spirit to use us in this kind of way.

Inspiring and diverse worship seemed sensible in principle. Often, however, this can be practically impossible to sustain with just one person being responsible for the whole thing. In many places we find one worship product. In practice people are asked to take it or leave it. If this is what leaders inherit, it is certainly much easier not to grapple with in the hope of ushering in change; to leave a single in-house style in place makes great sense from the point of view of clerical busyness and the total amount of work that there is to be done. Doing things differently, in terms of worship, would demand time of the minister, time that couldn't easily be found in the short-term.

When we do "bite the bullet" and decide to embrace a more diverse approach to worship, we find this gives us an opportunity to draw people further into the life of the church. If our approach to worship is narrow, so is the range of people who happily identify with it. When more and more people identify with diverse worship in this way, the church ends up having a breadth of contact with the local community that otherwise it couldn't. When people are allowed to use their gifts and coordinate the range of worship styles they believe it right to embrace, the number of people who really "identify" with church and its activities increases greatly. A warm, Jesus-centered spirituality can so often lead to loving relationships within the church. Surely, this is central to what we need to put in place in the parish. This too can be linked with small groups that meet to talk and share their faith in a safe, friendly environment. Such an approach would create a place where we could all learn to be church together and know that we are loved and accepted, even when we make mistakes in our faltering early steps in ministry, not to mention silly answers to questions we sometimes give in discussion groups. Fifty percent of the population are introverts and therefore do not function well in groups of over about eight people, yet, so often, as churches, we fail to recognize this and wonder why some people seem to sit quietly in corners never speaking at larger church events.

So many of us have difficulty just keeping our building going and feel we are swimming hard to keep afloat; therefore, evangelism is something of a scary word which we simply don't have the energy to contemplate. Without evangelism, of course, the church is not church but a private club for members only. Ultimately, it would be guaranteed to die. The Dead Sea, after all, is dead because it has insufficient inflow and outflow. A static ecclesiastical organization couldn't be any different.

Another challenge to us was the idea of useful structures in the life of the local church. So many of us have served on committees, both religious and secular, that seem to be there as something of an end in themselves—when in doubt, appoint another committee. Nothing can be more tedious and time-wasting as things go round and round in endless circles with no obvious end product. Was all this talk of MAPs (mission action planning) from the diocese and beyond just another committee or talking shop? Would anything useful come out of it all?

This all certainly gave us food for thought. Martyn initially went one Saturday to pray and chat these issues through with the two parish wardens and the lay reader, who at that time formed the leadership group of this parish. They began to realize that we did, indeed, need to fire on all cylinders if things were to move forward. Full involvement and lay ministry weren't to be undertaken as a "concession" to laypeople to keep them happy or in response to the reduction in the overall number of clerics in the wider church. All of this would be, instead, a response to the reality that the Spirit gives gifts and talents to all, for our great Creator remains creative amongst his people.

It was with excitement that they later fed back to the church council the need to form a mission committee. This would be a small working group tasked with working out what steps could be taken in order to work toward some of those "healthy" characteristics that we decided we wanted to claim as our own in this parish.

A Picture Begins to Emerge

As a parish, we were convinced about the characteristics of a healthy church. The church council discussed these at length and decided to set up a mission committee to explore how we could become a healthy church and eventually come up with a mission statement; without knowing what we really believed and were called to do, we would almost certainly end up getting nowhere, even if we were busy in the process. The mission group was to be set up for this purpose and then disbanded—already, we were aware of the danger of "jobs for life" that so often lead to committees and groups being established for their own sake. The church council decided to seek out a wide selection of church members for this group, not just the core people who already were very busy in the life of the parish. They decided to aim for balance when it came to age and gender too.

The group had six meetings, initially talking about what a healthy church should be and then moving on to look at where we would like to be as a parish in five years. They then slowly and with a certain excitement started putting into words things that were becoming important in the life of the church. This had to be in our own words and something that everybody in the parish could understand and make their own. This is the statement they prepared and which the church council were happy to endorse for our parish:

> We are part of the body of the Lord Jesus Christ, called to be his continuing presence in the world. As part of the worldwide Anglican Communion, our mission is to carry on his loving ministry and to fulfill his purpose. Therefore, the declared intent of the two churches of this parish is:
>
> - To proclaim the good news of the kingdom of God to all
>
> - To teach and baptize and to help strengthen the faith of all believers
>
> - To have the kind of worship and Christian education that enables people of all ages to better receive and know the Lord Jesus Christ.
>
> - To respond to the needs of all through loving service, to care for people in God's world who suffer, and to care for all that God has made
>
> - To be loving, caring family churches to which people would wish to belong

The church council discussed the statement at some length. Because the mission committee and the church council were drawn widely from the parish, we could be certain that the parish's mission statement reflected where the parish really stood; it wasn't, in any sense, "handed down" to people from on high by a ruling clique.

Calendars and bookmarks were produced carrying the statement. References were made to it in the preaching and teaching life of the church. As the statement reflected where we stood, it made sense to make it public on our parish website and notice boards.

The mission committee also reported back to the church council, an observation that was of crucial importance. If we were serious about remodeling the parish's life in the light of the statement, we would need to create new structures in our decision-making and ministry life in order to carry through what we now claimed as our vision and the good practice about which it spoke. The church council alone could never make it a reality.

We wrote to Bishop Barry, the Bishop of Llandaff, seeking his advice and guidance. He advised us not to make far-reaching decisions about these new structures until a new provincial and diocesan officer, Caroline Pascoe, had taken up her post and could walk with us as a parish. It is difficult to exaggerate the value of the help that Caroline gave us. She had come to us from Gloucester diocese and had a massive amount of experience in helping parishes there struggle with new ways of being church together. Caroline met with the church council, parish officers, and Martyn to help us steer clear of many of the errors that could easily have made.

What began to emerge in our discussions were a number of areas in which we would need to invest time, talents, and money if the mission statement was to become a reality for us. Caroline advised us to do a few things well rather than overload people and end up doing many things badly. In many ways, this was the hardest part, narrowing down so many ideas and things that we wanted to do. We had to decide which were the most important to us and, more importantly, which areas God wanted us to work in. We struggled in prayer and discussion with this as a church council for many months.

Finally, we decided on five areas in particular that we would concentrate on for a period of three years. After that, all groups would cease, and the process would start again. The five areas that we decided to work with were:

- Children
- Teenagers
- Setting up small groups for Bible study and fellowship
- A pastoral group called "the Church Beyond the Church"
- A team to coordinate the building project

We ended up adding a sixth group as we thought about the need for diversity in the worshipping life of the church. These were decisive steps for us as a church council and as a parish. In identifying these areas, we became aware that we would need to think about the gifts and abilities God had given to us; with God's help and Caroline's wisdom, people would soon be able to make a real contribution to different areas of the church's life in line with their gifts.

Not only were these decisions wise in themselves, they also echoed the teaching of Scripture. In Ephesians 4:1–16, we read how the ascended Christ gave gifts and abilities to his people. We were becoming convinced that we would need to take all of this seriously if we were to become the kind of church the Lord wanted us to be. We would need to think prayerfully about what God wanted us to do. We would also need to discern the kind of gifts he had given us as his people. These two tracks to our thinking and praying weren't contradictory in any sense, because God always gives us the things we need in order to fulfill his will. These were exciting and challenging days!

Flesh on the Bones

I t is quite a challenge to make our discussions and plans a reality, but that is what we were faced with as a church council. We had sought God's will as we narrowed down areas of ministry we felt he wanted us to be involved in. Now we would have to enter a stage of discernment.

The process of discernment linked our discussions and plans with the reality of making things that were important to us happen. Talk is cheap! Making decisions in the light of the things we believe in is where the rubber hits the road! It involved a process in which all of the people in church life identify those who are gifted to exercise various ministries in these new areas. Here, in particular, Caroline's wisdom, born of experience, was invaluable.

Having decided the areas we needed to take particularly seriously as a parish, the church council decided to move the whole process decisively forward one Sunday morning in September. Instead of the two morning communions held at different churches in the parish, we met together for a single act of worship. The original idea had been for Martyn to lead this on his return from Jerusalem. Having needed to take to his bed ill on his return—thankfully, you don't need the details—one of our church council members led this for us. On reflection, it seemed to us that God had been involved in the details of this whole process, as having a parishioner to lead us on this particular Sunday morning sent an important message to all present: we weren't looking for parishioners to help the minister; we were looking for the baptized to exercise their ministries together in the body of Christ.

During this service, we thought prayerfully about two things: the areas of ministry and who might be approached to help us in each of these, and our gifts and abilities as individuals. Two sheets of paper (see Appendix 1 and 2) were given to each member of the congregation.

It had been made clear that this exercise was not a vote, with the "winners" approached and the "losers" left where they were. Throughout all of this, we were looking for ways for people to be active in the life of the parish to the extent that they and their brothers and sisters in Christ thought would be appropriate. We were thrilled beyond measure with the way this turned out. In all of this, God had managed to blend together, in what he was doing among us, those who had been present in church for just a short time with those who had never lived in any other parish.

On the first form, we used the prayerful silence to think about work with preteens, small groups, and so on; we jotted down people's names under each heading as they came to mind. These were to be the people who made up each small group. This was very much a prayerful reflection of people's God-given gifts, not simply a process in which we voted for our friends.

On the second sheet, we thought of people, their gifts and abilities. This tended to confirm the picture that emerged on the first form. It also gave the parish the opportunity to earmark certain people who were overwhelmingly recognized to have leadership skills. These would be approached to chair one of the areas of ministry the church council had earlier identified; they would be brought together to serve on the ministry development team (MDT) with Martyn to help coordinate the parish's work as a whole. In this way, the church council's vision, enshrined in the mission statement, could begin to become a reality. This would allow us to set up new structures that, in turn, would help us to sustain good practice across half a dozen important areas of ministry. Without these new structures, the parish's mission statement would be no more than wishful thinking.

After this Sunday morning, Martyn met together with Caroline to collate and sift all the forms that had been filled in. Under the guidance of the Spirit, the parish had overwhelmingly identified those who could be approached for membership of the MDT and the six areas of ministry, including the development of our worship life. Martyn chaired the worship development group, as this functioned very differently from the others and later would develop into a group alongside the ministry development team.

The vast majority of those who were approached accepted, knowing that they were being asked to serve for a three-year period. Almost always, the small number of those who felt that they wouldn't be able to help at this stage in the parish's development cited changes in their family circumstances. In some cases, when we went through this whole process again three years later, they were then in a position to help. Initially, we just contacted the people who would lead each small group and form the MDT. Members of the MDT would later be given lists of the people that the whole congregation had identified as having gifts in each area. The leader of that group would approach their new team members.

At this stage, none of us really knew how all of this would work out in practice; that would come later. It was with some trepidation that some people accepted the invitation to serve, for most this was very much a leap of faith but a leap of faith that, when taken, was to help them grow in ministry, faith, and confidence. There was much we didn't know at that stage. What we did know was that God had helped to put flesh on the bones of the parish's vision; we were ready to begin to move forward.

The people of God in the Old Testament knew what it was to see ministry and leadership as things that were shared throughout Israel. In Numbers 11:16–17, we read of God pouring himself out upon seventy elders so that they could minister alongside Moses; it would be together that God's people would be able to move forward. They would need to grapple with issues of unity in the wilderness. They would not be able to enter the Promised Land without it. It would be together, as God's people in the parish, that we would be able to enter into ours!

See Appendix 1 and 2 for samples of the forms we used.

The Ministry Development Team

Our first ministry development team (MDT) meeting was held with excitement and some apprehension. This was new territory for all of us, and no one quite knew what to expect. The title of the group was deliberately chosen; a title can say a great deal. This group was not the group that did the entire ministry for the parish. Rather, it was the group that was tasked with helping all of us develop our God-given ministry. It was also important that this group was a team; after all, areas of ministry overlap, and turf wars were the last thing we wanted. We needed good, healthy relationships, as we were all working towards the same goal.

Caroline, the diocesan officer, sat in on the first meeting and many afterward to guide and advise us. It proved useful to have someone with experience walking alongside us in these new areas. She often asked questions and made observations; hers was not a style that turned up to our meetings with a blueprint in the briefcase. Our parish, and therefore MDT, like all other parishes that seek new patterns of ministry, was unique; we needed to find God's will for us.

Each MDT meeting started with worship, a short time prepared in advance by one of the group—we took turns in this. It was so important to remind ourselves that God was at the center of all we did; God was the guide of our activities and planning. The MDT wasn't just one more committee convened for its own sake. A lighted candle then burned throughout the meeting, a visible reminder of God's presence among us.

We quickly decided on a layperson to chair the meetings, particularly as we had a person with amazing gifts in the area of helping us look together for ways to navigate these uncharted waters; he was someone who helped us think and stretched our imaginations. Someone else took notes to produce minutes so we could recall the ground we had covered and things we'd decided; note-taking was crucial for us, as our next MDT meeting sometimes wouldn't take place for a few months. Already, this group was modeling all-member ministry, with people leading worship, chairing meetings, and taking minutes.

At the first meeting, we emphasized that this group was set up at the church council's request and answered to the church council. This needed to be seen as an expression of our understanding of church. The group existed to implement the church council's vision. It, therefore, frequently reported back to the church council, keeping them fully informed of developments. Any major initiative was taken to the church council for approval (such as the new building project). The church council showed its support of the MDT in a very practical way. It agreed that each group within the MDT would receive $250 for their work, a practical expression of the wider parish's interest in what was taking place at these meetings.

Each member of the MDT was to chair his or her own group. We had quite a lengthy discussion about what to call these groups and decided on "coordinating teams." The implication, again, was of teamwork and encouraging everyone's ministry, not one person or group doing everything. We then had the task of going through the lists from the discernment process and deciding who had gifts in each different area to serve on these coordinating teams. Each person ended up with a list of three or four people to contact to serve on their team.

Each coordinator met with the team they set up. These teams would make plans which were then fed back to the MDT for approval and discussion. This kept good order. Sometimes, we found that the groups and their plans overlapped, so they could work together; at other times, events and plans clashed, so we would change or adapt them. None of the ground we covered during these years would have been possible without our new structures. They also took away the potential sense of isolation and total responsibility from the teams and their leaders; what emerged instead was a sense of shared ministry across the parish.

Caroline reminded us as an MDT that it is better to do one thing well than try to do too many and achieve nothing. This was passed on to the coordinating groups too. We needed to remember in everything we did that people are already very busy. Many of us have considerable responsibilities and duties apart from our church lives. Overburdening people and wearing them out was neither useful nor the kind of thing God would want.

The busyness of our parishioners was remembered when it came to training too. We needed the best resources we could find from the wider church; that was true. Training and the encouragement of people were important as well. On the other hand, bearing in mind that people can often be overstretched before they even think about their church commitments, we found that attending courses offered centrally by the diocese could often be too much for us to ask of them. We then decided on training that would be delivered in our locality, sometimes perhaps with neighboring parishes. On other occasions, courses would be offered in-house, within the parish, as these might involve a commitment of an evening rather than a whole day away. We also started to build up a library of books and other resources that people could borrow.

The MDT felt it was important to include the whole congregation in ministry development. We produced prayer sheets for people to use when decisions were taken, asking the whole congregation to pray as we moved forward and activities started. Notice boards at both churches had a diagram (see Appendix 3) of the new structures and names of the people serving on each group so that everyone was aware of what was happening and also of who to contact if they wanted to get involved themselves or feed in ideas for our new groups to discuss. Openness was to be the watchword for us. We also emphasized that church council meetings were open to the entire congregation so that they could sit in and listen; church council minutes of meetings were made available so that everyone knew what was going on.

In all of this, we rightly placed a great deal of

emphasis on the ministry of all the baptized and tried, at all costs, to avoid the reality of establishing "jobs for life" or setting up an "elite group" of empowered people with others simply playing the part of onlookers. Now anybody who wished to be actively involved in the life of the parish could do so. We deliberately thought and prayed through the entire congregation to check that no one was left out who was willing to be appropriately involved. It didn't matter how long people had been in church with us; we were all invited to become involved. In many respects, there is no better way to really welcome new people to the church's life than to invite them to pray and work alongside others. On the whole, people responded with considerable enthusiasm and immediately felt at home among us. In the Letter of James (2:26), we are reminded that genuine faith in Christ expresses itself in practical ways, in the things we do day in day out. Newcomers to church joined the rest of us in learning that lesson and putting it into practice.

Diverse Worship That Inspires

Because of the central place that worship would occupy, we couldn't wait until we had put all of the new structures in place before turning our attention to it. At the same time, as we were setting up the new ministry structures, therefore, we were also seriously looking at developing our worship life together. We had been challenged by the New Wine conference idea of "inspiring and diverse worship" but knew we had a long way to go in order to achieve that. We knew that one busy Minister could not develop worship and sustain it on their own. We decided that this area was important to us, so we added it to the MDT from the outset. Though it would operate a little differently from the other groups that were part of the MDT, it would nevertheless be accountable to both the MDT and the church council in the same way as all the others.

Anglicanism/Episcopalianism allows for a large measure of diversity of worship. It has over the centuries. What was taking place among us as we worshiped was very much in the spirit of Anglicanism as we understood it. For example, we continued to value communion services on Sundays and midweek, and these took their place alongside morning and evening prayer and other forms of worship. A neighboring church had started a course for worship leaders; it was natural for us to seek their advice and to draw encouragement from what they were doing.

Now that we had decided to press ahead in this area, we needed to pick worship leaders. Obviously, these had to have a living spirituality, they had to be team players, and also they had to be representative of the whole congregation in terms of its breadth of spirituality. Ultimately, God helped us through the process of discerning those whom it would be appropriate to approach as potential worship leaders. We prayed on many occasions while mentally looking up and down each pew in the church at the people who sat in them. God then brought to our minds people who we might have easily over looked. We deliberately put in a cross section of the congregations both in terms of age and worship preference so that the whole congregation was represented and could later be catered for.

About twenty people initially were approached and asked to be worship leaders. This was very much a leap of faith for us all, as at that stage we had no idea what this would develop into or how it would work in practice. We simply started where we were and with our group of willing but somewhat apprehensive people who were prepared to commence a worship training course. The vicar of the nearby parish, who had worship leaders in his own church, kindly offered to come and lead our course. We used a simple but effective course by SEAN that arose out of Evangelical Anglican circles in Latin America. The course provided a study book and a workbook for each person and taught about good and bad practice, plus the various ingredients that help make up appropriate, balanced worship. During these teaching sessions, there was, frankly, a certain amount of panic in evidence and many questions asked as we launched out upon new and unknown waters. How amazing it was later to see these same people growing and developing their ministries as they stepped out in faith.

The group was diverse in what type of worship they would naturally feel at home with but also in how publicly involved they wished to be during services. Some people wanted to help prepare a service but did not want to do anything in public, which was fine; others were happy to lead the whole service, including preparing and delivering their own meditation material; many others were in between the two extremes. Shy and extrovert people therefore could each find their place and feel comfortable.

Nobody was forced to do anything they weren't comfortable with; rather, each was gently encouraged to fulfill their potential. We have, however, watched as people have grown in confidence. Some stepped out initially and did relatively small things, such as a reading, yet, over the years, their faith and confidence grew to the point where they were happy to move on to attempt things that would ask more of them. We began to see people developing gifts in certain areas. Some might naturally operate in the area of informal family worship while others had a natural flair for worship in the traditional language Prayer Book tradition. Shorter services or services with relatively few people present proved to be a safe training ground where they could find encouragement as they helped alongside others, and all of this without judgment or condemnation. Rather, as active participation in worship was something so many were involved in, the worship leaders developed some of the positive characteristics of a support group; we were all in this together. Each tottering step was encouraged and applauded by others, which helped build confidence.

The fact that we now had a group of willing worship leaders meant that we were able to broaden the type of services that we could make available in the parish. We were able to sustain four fairly different approaches to worship, in fact.

Our Sunday morning communion at the parish church had a high level of involvement from people, yet this intentionally retained a more traditional feel. At our other church, once a month, we incorporated drama and all sorts of other ingredients into our celebration of communion, giving it a more family-centered feel. Prayer Book worship became our third stream, with fortnightly evensong and a midweek communion; the intention was that this would continue to play an important role in our life together. A new 6:30 p.m. service also began. This was very informal, with no set weekly pattern at all. Modern worship songs required the use of guitar, sometimes percussion, and keyboards. The words of the songs were put on an overhead projector, which sometimes was used for illustrating talks.

People were encouraged to come to whichever type of service they found most helpful rather than to wear themselves out trying to come to everything. Initially, two worship leaders were asked to plan services together;

this built confidence and helped people share ideas as they worked together. The spin-off effect in all of this was the deepening of friendship and fellowship.

As all the worship leaders were busy people, we were aware that it wasn't wise to ask too much of any single person. As a group, we decided ongoing training would be important to us, but, for the same reason, this would be one evening every three months or so. In these sessions, the group itself set the agenda and decided the topics that would be covered. Martyn usually led these sessions at first, although there was a high level of group participation each time. As the months went on, others led the times of training. We looked at areas such as voice projection and practical areas concerned with the leading of worship. Much time was also spent looking together at biblical topics and themes. The worship leaders built up a library of reference books that could be borrowed during times of service preparation; these include biblical commentaries, prayer books, and drama books, and a host of others.

At the outset, we mentioned that we couldn't wait for all of our new ministry and decision-making structures to be in place before setting out on the kind of changes that were required in our worship life. What happened instead was that worship played its part in shaping us as God's people and making us the kind of people who would be prepared to walk with the Lord in the other new things he was asking us to do. Without meeting God in this way in worship, we probably wouldn't have had the courage to say "yes" to change in other areas of our life together.

This whole area of worship was later to be developed further, but the initial, first steps were, by this stage, in place. We were able to set out tentatively in the direction of diverse worship and to sustain this week in, week out in a way we could not have thought of doing before. These were exciting days!

Church Night

From the beginning of our time in the parish, we had been firm believers in raising the spiritual temperature of the church's life. This was done, in part, through the teaching and preaching that took place in the context of Sunday worship. Early on, however, we came to the conclusion that this, on its own, wasn't enough; we would need to teach the Christian faith midweek as well.

This was done on a fortnightly basis on Wednesday evenings in sessions we called "church night." The idea was that whatever our preferred style of worship, be it traditional or less formal, these midweek teaching sessions were for all of us. Church night was intended to provide something of a focus for our life together in the parish.

We attempted to include characteristics of the parish's different worship styles into what we did together on these occasions. The first fifteen minutes or so would be given to worship. Sometimes, this would be the singing of well-known hymns; at other times, more charismatic worship material or meditative songs would be used. Different people would lead the singing and play organ, guitar, or keyboards on a rota basis. A more liturgical style of worship played its part alongside the others as well. This was a way of attempting to recognize the unity we share in Christ; our diversity was a gift from God rather than something to be eradicated—it was intended to enrich us rather than divide us. Over the years, the teaching of the faith was delivered in different ways too. More often than not, there was a talk for about fifteen minutes at the most. After this, we went into groups to discuss questions that had been prepared on the theme beforehand. On other occasions, the teaching itself was done in groups as we shared our views and insights. This again was a way of seeing the differences among us as a strength rather than a weakness.

People grew in their faith through these occasions, as they had an opportunity to share their experiences and different ways of understanding things with others. In fact, it was this component of a church night evening that people seemed to value most. In this way, we were able to take seriously the fact that the Holy Spirit leads the whole church into all truth. Each of us had an active role to play in understanding the Christian faith and teaching it to others. It was important for us all to spend time listening to God as he spoke through others. For many, group discussions were a new experience and one that they came to enjoy a great deal.

Martyn didn't take part in the discussion groups, as having a minister present in a small group isn't always an advantage. Some discussion groups treat the minister as a guest expert. The danger with this is that instead of sharing and exploring ideas from their own experience the minister is consulted, as often as not, for the "correct" answer to whatever question is under discussion. A huge amount of fun was a byproduct of time spent talking in this way. Fellowship was deepened as we enjoyed this expression of being church together. These discussion times seemed to flow quite naturally as we chatted together over tea and coffee.

On occasions, the evening's teaching time was brought to a close with an opportunity to feed back to the whole group some of the insights that had surfaced in discussion. This too proved fun, as groups joked with each other about some of the things that emerged in the discussions of other groups.

Church night too was to be a good training ground for many of us. Different people were asked to read from the Bible in public—some had never done this before, but felt safer trying in a small group setting; reading for the first time on a Sunday would have been much more daunting. Most of the people attending were asked to prepare and deliver prayers in whatever style they chose. This, as well as being a good training ground, also meant that we all benefited from different styles and types of prayer. In time, some worship leaders were also happy to lead the group discussions. Again, each of us grew as we encountered new practices and insights for the first time.

These sessions covered a great deal of ground over the years. There were series on the teaching of Jesus, the nature of worship, the fruit of the Spirit (from Galatians chapter five), and heroes in the Old Testament. We also looked at the Prophets and Psalms. It seemed to us that church night was a better place to do consistent teaching using series of talks than a Sunday morning.

God seemed to have used these Wednesday evening sessions to reinforce an important lesson about taking a lead from him as well. We initially had the idea for church night when we had been in the parish for less than a year. The idea seemed sensible enough. Surely, God would want us to understand our faith more. That being obviously true, we couldn't imagine why it shouldn't be established there and then. The idea bombed; it didn't happen. In fact, these sessions didn't commence for another two or three years. We had to learn that there is all the difference in the world between a bright idea and something God was asking us to do. Instead, church night was to have small beginnings as a home study group.

During church night sessions, we grew in our own faith as well as in our understanding of the Christian faith. Without these times, we would all have been the poorer. In many ways, it would have been difficult without them to continue the journey together on which we had embarked. These sessions continue today. They have shown us that we express our desire to seek God when we study the Scriptures together. God inspired these writings (2 Timothy 3:16). When we take them seriously, we take him seriously.

Small Groups
Coordinating Team

The church council had asked this team to set up small groups across the parish for friendship and fellowship. How to achieve this was left up to the team.

The group met several times to pray and chat through the best way to achieve this. It came to the conclusion that it might be best first to cover the basics of Christianity as a church by doing an Alpha course. This would also get people more familiar with the idea of small friendship groups for discussion and fellowship. They decided that the first Alpha course was to be for existing church members. It was important that we all had the opportunity to renew our faith and share together.

As a parish, we had never run an Alpha course before, so we turned to a nearby parish for advice. Their Alpha team was happy to meet with the small group coordinating team in order to offer advice and tips. This proved very useful; often, what works well in a large London parish may not work equally well in every part of Wales. We realized that we would have to tailor the course to our own situation whilst leaving the substance of it intact.

We bought and read the many useful Alpha course guidebooks. One person attended the Alpha conference and came back full of ideas and suggestions. We also talked widely to people we knew who had run or attended Alpha courses. In all this, we had decided to prepare fully rather than just rush ahead.

Eventually, we were ready and able to hand out invitations to the Alpha course to each person in church. We tried, where possible, to talk to people and invite them personally, giving us a chance to answer any questions they may have had. One tip we had picked up was to have a number of people praying for the Alpha course during the sessions. We did this quite openly and explained, during the sessions, that others were meeting at the same time to pray for us.

We did not have the facilities for extensive catering at that stage, so each session began with coffee and light refreshments rather than anything more elaborate. People were encouraged to sit at the same tables each week to build up friendships. The Alpha principle of giving of our best in everything is a good one. On each table, we had tablecloths and fresh flowers; our best china was used, and good, light refreshments were provided to show that God and others deserve the best we can give. Our first course had a good attendance, with people sitting around four tables learning to share their faith with each other as trust began to build.

For the discussion group leaders, this was also an excellent training ground. Many of us had never done anything like this before and so took on the task with some fears. Others helped to welcome people as they arrived for the sessions, with more again helping with the catering. In a small way, we began modeling every member ministry in this way, with different gifts being used according to people's abilities. There were plenty of opportunities for everyone who wanted to get involved. We all found the running of the course to be a lot of hard work. It required high levels of commitment from us, yet the results were well worth the effort.

At the end of the first course, each person was given a leaflet inviting them to join a home study group (cell group) in the parish so that they could continue to enjoy the small group fellowship they had found. Due to the response, we were able to set up four cell groups in the parish.

There were already two afternoon ladies' meetings, and they both felt that once a month they would like to study the cell group material together. Two new evening cells were added. The invitation to join one of these went out to the whole parish, not just the people who had attended the Alpha course.

The small group coordinating team tried to encourage people to lead and take part in the cell groups. It, however, remained a support network in the background, organizing dates and producing study material. We produced a pack for each cell group leader, giving a suggested time frame for a session, some prayers to begin and end with, a song sheet with a CD of music, and study material. The study material contained a small amount of teaching to read out and questions to be used for discussion.

The marvelous thing with these new structures is that nothing is set in stone, so the coordinating teams, with the MDT's agreement, had the freedom to change and adapt. In many ways, this team had achieved the aim that the church council had set out for it. In time to come, beyond the life of the first MDT, this coordinating team would continue to monitor and assist the cells in the parish. However, as this initial period came to a close, the team felt that Alpha was so important in helping people renew their faith or come to faith for the first time that we would need to set up an evangelism coordinating team that would then oversee subsequent Alpha courses.

The small groups coordinating team ran a second and third Alpha course during its three years in place. This time, the course was advertised in order to reach people in the parish beyond our existing congregations. Invitations to the courses went through every door in the parish on the front page of our magazine. Posters were displayed in local shops. Though the response to this type of advertising was not massive, we did end up with subsequent courses being attended by a mixture of church attendees and people from the wider community.

All of this was to prove to be beneficial in a number of ways. We saw some people growing in their faith; others came to faith for the first time. As a result, a few new people joined the church, and this was an encouragement to us all, not least to members of the coordinating team that had overseen all of this. As each course drew to a close, people were invited to join cell groups to continue their study and fellowship.

As a team, we were learning an important lesson: whilst we didn't have a blueprint on which we could rely, we did have a God who would lead and direct us. We were also learning by experience, even in small and mundane things such as how much food an Alpha course would require. Flexibility seemed to be the key in all of this! In the book of Exodus, the Israelites were asked to keep in step with God as they journeyed through the wilderness. When God asked them to stop, they stopped; when he asked them to set out, they set out. The truth is that we never get to a place in our faith where we can dispense with this kind of step-by-step obedience to the Lord. The trouble starts when we think we have outgrown this approach because we have come to the view that we have a blueprint instead.

Youth Coordinating Team

Most Christians would agree that working with young people is not easy. Filling pews with smiling teens remains a challenge for us all!

In our early years in the parish, we had started a youth group that met at the rectory once a month. Most evenings, this began with Christian teaching followed by pizza and the watching of a film. A friend and colleague, who was then the youth chaplain for our diocese, had found that this kind of approach worked in his own parish. This gave our young people a strong friendship group, one that met at other times for social events. However, we both knew that leading young people wasn't something for which either of us had a particular flair. That illustrates, again, why we needed new structures with more and more people ministering side by side; the minister and spouse are not gifted in every area of ministry, and we are all damaged when we plan as if they are. We need to admit this and seek out others who do have a relevant gifting from God.

The youth coordinating team contained a group

of people who loved working with young people and were highly gifted. They met and planned with great enthusiasm.

Initially, they decided to work with the group of teens that already met once a month, to build on the friendships that were emerging. They decided to use a young people's service that had been produced with this sort of group in mind. This encouraged participation from all concerned and left plenty of space for discussion. Pizzas were then served, and the new pattern of diverse worship the parish had embraced gave the teens the option to stay on for informal worship at 6:30. They were encouraged to take part in the church's worship life, often doing dramas or readings at services in our other worship streams. In addition, they planned and took part during informal worship on Christmas Eve and Good Friday. These were always popular events and were especially helpful in attracting families from the local community. Many of these young people have now left to attend university. They continued to meet for films and pizza during the holidays.

In common with many Anglican/Episcopalian parishes, we tend to "lose" many children from regular church attendance once they reach comprehensive school (11–18 year olds). We haven't found that an easy nut to crack. The teen's coordinating team decided to start something for children in the last year of junior school (10 and 11 year olds) in order to encourage them to continue in active church attendance. This continued until we closed our parish hall in Alltwen to build the new church.

It has been interesting to see how diverse teenagers themselves are in their worship preferences. It is easy to stereotype teenagers and believe that they all like the same "product." However, the fact is that as they enjoy all sorts of different music, activities, films, etc; they also warm to different types of worship. With the exception of Prayer Book liturgy, we have teenagers who come to all other types of service. That's as it should be. Some of them have a spirituality that would be broadly evangelical; of these, a number might be happy with charismatic worship, but a number would not. That underlines the importance of the young people's group being fully involved in making decisions about how they relate to church life. It is not desirable that any of us, young or not, should be cast in the role of passive consumers of a product that is determined and delivered by others.

The Preteens
Coordinating Team

This team also had a daunting task ahead of them! Sunday school work with this age group had become a feature of the parish's life for a number of years. Bearing in mind that children's work rightly demands a massive amount of time on the part of those who are involved in it, it was crucial that this team thought carefully about the direction it should take. From the start, they were convinced that it is important to do a few things well rather than burn out trying to sustain a massive programme of activity.

Firstly, the team reviewed where we were as a parish in this area of its life. As a result of this and discussions at the MDT and the church council, it was agreed that we started a more informal, family-centered communion service once a month. As this was helped by the worship leaders' team, we were becoming aware of the fact that our coordinating teams often overlapped and needed to work well together. From time to time, a worship leader would assist in the service, with children taking part in many ways—sometimes with the leading of prayers, with readings, or with a drama on the overall theme of that day.

The preteen's coordinating team felt quite strongly that children not being able to receive communion, though they are baptized, was a problem which we needed to look at as a parish. Liaising with the church council, they discussed the issues involved and made recommendations to the MDT and the church council. As a result of this, we contacted our bishop in order to get advice about how we could move forward in this area. He gave permission for us to be one of the parishes in the diocese in which children were allowed to prepare to receive communion before they were confirmed (often in early teens).

The preteen's team took this onboard and gave much thought to preparing a course for the children to follow. The team decided that it would be good for the children to study together at Sunday school, which met during the first part of morning worship. The group helped us as a parish to make the necessary changes in order to welcome young children in this way. It then helped us in the planning of a service of first communion, bringing a celebration cake for the refreshments after the service. In this way, our new structures weren't simply the result of our desire to embrace new patterns of ministry in church. In turn, they helped us make further changes to our lives together in Christ.

The team had helped us as a parish to think afresh about the importance of baptism as the point of entry into the life of the family of God. We were coming to realize that there was something fundamentally wrong about part of the family not being invited to the family meal, the communion. Children are now taken to be an integral part of our church life. They are fully part of the church of today, rather than members in waiting of the church of tomorrow. When children are pushed to the margins, we are all the poorer. Certainly, as we look at the ministry of Jesus, it becomes clear that our younger people are still to be welcomed into the kingdom of God and have an important place in the lives of the people of God.

This coordinating team also did preparatory work for us looking at working with children once the new St. John's church had opened. This has been borne in mind by those who are helping to oversee the building project for us. It has become important to us that our new church at the Alltwen end of the parish would include a café and all other features that would help us provide a safe place for little ones to meet. During this period in our life together in church, as we attempted to move forward as we knew we should, a number of our coordinating teams worked together (those concerned with our work with teens, preteens, the building project, and worship leaders) and this with the assistance of the MDT and the church council itself. All of this would have been inconceivable without us being prepared to embrace new patterns of decision-making and ministry. The changes we were making would have been impossible had there even been a hint of empire-building or turf wars in our life together. The body of Christ, here, was learning to minister and work together in ways that were certainly new for us. Had the spiritual temperature not been warmed at the outset, this would not have happened. This ultimately wasn't simply an exercise in management and new ways of doing things. If it wasn't about God and what he wanted to do in us and among us, nothing would have been possible at all.

The Church beyond the Church

As the church council had discussed the areas we would need to take seriously over this three-year period, one thing cropped up in the discussions a number of times. That was the importance of caring for people in the wider community.

This proved to be both exciting and challenging. What was envisaged here was something that was different from evangelism. We were obviously clear about the importance of reaching out into the community in order to commend the good news of Jesus. This wasn't being challenged or removed in any way. What we were looking at here, by contrast, was a growing sense that we should simply try to care for others, with no ulterior motive being present; it didn't matter whether those in need had any connections with church or not. We were attempting to build on something that many people in the parish had been involved in individually over many years. We were trying to care, because that is what Jesus would do.

This particular coordinating team helped us as a parish to do a number of things in the wider community, things, again, that we probably wouldn't have done without the new structures.

We visited nursing and residential homes in the area to sing carols in the period leading up to Christmas. Other events were held at a sheltered housing scheme in the parish. In addition to this, cards were printed in order to welcome people who had moved into the neighborhood. These were made available at the back of church. Members of the congregations were encouraged to deliver them to newcomers to the area as part of the church's welcome to them.

From time to time, contact was made with bereaved friends or neighbors in the community. Sometimes, they expressed an interest in coming to a church event or service; lifts were then offered.

A certain amount of visiting of those who were ill had been done by church members over a number of years. The coordinating team also helped us to expand this by setting up a trained group of visitors called "parish friends." People had been approached and invited to get involved on the strength of what had been written on our two forms during the discernment process (Appendix 1 and 2). This element of discernment by the church was highly important. It ensured that only those widely recognized to have the necessary gifts were invited to take part.

Once the parish friends scheme was set up, training was offered. This might, on occasion, be with a local parish that was setting up something similar, or it might be done by ourselves two or three times a year in our parish hall. General guidelines were offered as a fruit of the good practice of those who had been involved in this kind of work over a long period of time. Appendix 4 shows the kind of information that was discussed at various training sessions we held, as people contributed their own wisdom and good advice. In this way, people found that they were able to play an active part in the training we offered. In turn, this built confidence and helped encourage church members about the number of gifts and insights they were in a position to share with others. The pastoral visiting, as part of this scheme, was appreciated by a significant number of people.

At meetings of this coordinating team, many suggestions were made about things we could begin in this area. The maturity of this group helped it to decide which of them should be implemented and which should be left, at least for the time being. Especially in this type of work, it is easy to attempt a huge number of tasks and become exhausted in the process without seeing anything through to completion. What we wanted as a church was to establish ministry we could sustain, bearing in mind the needs of those who were kind enough to get involved.

The church beyond the church coordinating team was on a journey. So was the parish as a whole. As various things were tried, our understanding of what God wanted us to do and the things that really mattered to us got clearer. For all of us, these years were an example of learning by doing; this team helped the parish understand that we often grow in our service of God as we practice ministry and allow God to guide us step-by-step in the things we do. This group helped us lay foundations that we were later to build on when our new church was opened.

The Building Project

Closing a church can be a difficult and distressing thing to do at the best of times. A couple of years before the ministry development team had been set up, the church council had been praying about the right way forward for one of its two churches (St. John the Baptist in Alltwen). A significant amount of money had been spent repairing St. John's over a long period of time. The end result was that at least another $150,000 would be needed in order to keep the building in use, with the Disability Discrimination Act due to come into effect in about a year's time.

This was significant for us as a parish because St. John's was a fairly large and very cold Victorian church with no kitchen and no usable toilet. It was situated on the side of a very steep hill on one side of the Swansea Valley. Access was far from easy for able-bodied people; for those with additional difficulties, access was absolutely impossible. We set up a group to study possible disabled access, and they reported back to the church council about possible ways forward in the light of legislation governing public buildings and Health and Safety issues. In the light of this, we recognized that no new solution to the issue of access would be possible. The church council reluctantly came to a realization that the building, though much loved by us and many in the wider community, might need to be closed.

It was with an eye to the future and the church's mission that the church council asked the fabric committee of the parish to produce a feasibility study document about the building to help us look at possible ways forward. We realized that even if funding could be secured to repair the Victorian building, our needs were no longer Victorian needs. Much more would be required of a church building in that part of the parish if our emerging vision was to be realized. It was with heavy hearts that members of the church council, some of whom had been baptized and married there, voted unanimously to close the building and to redevelop the parish hall that stood right at the heart of the community.

One of the MDT's coordinating teams was formed to handle the redevelopment and extension of the parish hall. This group needed to cover a huge amount of ground if we were to end up with a new St. John's in Alltwen with appropriate facilities right at the heart of that part of our local community.

The whole community had been consulted via a questionnaire in order to discover what kind of facilities would best meet the needs of people who lived in the area. Applications for grants were made to a massive number of grant-making bodies. It would be difficult to exaggerate the amount of time all of this took. The group's coordinator held countless meetings with the parish's architect and quantity surveyor in order to help the church council decide which of a range of possible drawings for the newly extended building should be accepted, and this in the light of the amount of funding that looked likely to be secured.

Again, none of this would have been possible without the parish's new structures. No church council could have devoted this amount of time to the rebuild scheme, and if it did, everything else would have to have come to a grinding halt. New patterns of ministry and decision-making are not simply a hobby for parts of the church of Christ with a particular interest in these things. They were central to our life together and to the kinds of things we were able to do.

The whole enterprise was bathed in prayer. Those who came to worship and to church council meetings were well aware that if we weren't walking in step with God in this part of our life, things would never work out as they should. We were convinced as a parish that we didn't want fundraising to dominate our life, as it easily could. The emphasis instead would be on applications to grant-making bodies by the relevant coordinating team and on prayer and the ongoing mission of the church for all of us.

It was essential that this group was part of the MDT, as the new building would be so important to each other group and to the kind of ministry they would want to consider in the future. It meant that many people across the parish were able to feed their needs back to the team planning the new building in order that it would have appropriate facilities.

We asked members of the neighborhood about the type of building they would like to see. We discussed our needs amongst the various parish groups; the youth group was consulted and their views noted as well. After much discussion and prayer, planning began. The old hall would become our new worship space, with the option of part of this area being used for the kind of events that would previously have been held in the parish hall. As we planned, many things would need to be moveable or stackable. In addition, a new better-equipped kitchen was planned. Two new rooms would be added, one as a prayer room/smaller church, the other as a café/meeting room. The needs of those who are disabled were borne in mind in many ways, not only in respect of access itself. We tried to plan for ourselves as a church with our own diverse collection of needs and requirements, plus those of the wider community.

As the plans were being clarified by the church council and the funds were being secured, there was a feeling amongst church members that they wanted to have an opportunity to contribute individually to the project. A gift day was arranged for one Easter Day. Money would be brought as part of the people's worship, and this, itself, would end up making a real contribution to the building of a new St. John's.

The only part of the site of the old St. John's that would be retained was the interment of ashes plot, with a new entrance leading up to it. It was of crucial importance that this was handled with as much sensitivity as possible, as many people in the community who identified with the church in various ways had loved ones buried there. It was the wish of the church council that people would still be able to visit the site to think, reflect, and pray.

By the time this particular team came to the end of its three-year term, the realization of the project was practically in sight. Work would soon be able to commence, and the realization of the parish's vision had taken a giant step forward.

Thanks to this particular coordinating team and the assistance it gave to the church council, there was a real sense of excitement among us all about the possibilities that lay ahead. We were coming to regard God not as a distant One who was to be served but as our Father who wanted the best for his children. We were planning for good things to happen, believing that God wanted nothing less.

The Minister's Role Changes

When new structures and ways of ministering are embraced by a church, the members find themselves on a steep learning curve. They are not alone in this, however, for the minister also has much to learn. He or she will almost certainly have been trained for a different type of ministry in years gone by and will have to come to terms with a whole host of new expectations and challenges. When a church starts to fire on all cylinders, however, there is no alternative; the priest has to be an agent for change or may become, unintentionally, an obstacle in the way ahead.

This is the case because more work is being sustained by more people in more areas of church life. The landscape will have changed for the minister too. The cleric's ministry and leadership role couldn't possibly just carry on as if nothing had happened.

About halfway through the life of the first ministry development team, Martyn went on a course in Derbyshire with diocesan colleagues. A group was there from Derby diocese, teaching at a workshop about the new patterns of ministry that had been embraced there. This helped things click into place for him in many ways.

Their experience was that two things happened when new patterns were practiced in the parishes of Derby diocese. The first was that parishioners—the baptized—started to exercise their own priestly ministry; the second was that ministers started to embrace a more episcopal, overseeing type of role. This undoubtedly is what was beginning to happen among us in the parish. It wasn't that Martyn was simply becoming a manager but was ministering in a new way alongside parishioners as active colleagues.

Many things can be said about this new role for the minister. What couldn't be said was that this was some kind of abdication of leadership on the minister's part. When new patterns of ministry are embraced, no one, least of all the cleric, is called to sit back and simply watch the activity of others. In many ways, Martyn will never have been busier in the parish, but the busyness had a different and more productive pattern.

It is fair to say that this is a more active, hands-on style of leadership, as the minister interacts with people as they grow in ministry. Like ministers, they themselves make their own mistakes and must be allowed to do so. We grow by learning and doing. The only way to avoid making mistakes is to do nothing, and this is the greatest mistake of all.

With more worship taking place, the cleric may be present at more services and will certainly need to remain alert to the many good things and occasional less helpful things that may be going on. His/her preaching and teaching ministry will need to expand so that input can appropriately be given in many different types of services.

More pastoral work will be carried out by many more people as well. Again, the cleric will need to monitor things, offering help and advice. This was in line with remarks made by Archbishop Barry at a previous residential clergy school in Worcester: the priest may not be doing the pastoral work directly but was directly involved in making sure that pastoral work was being done.

Perhaps the minister's learning curve is steeper than that of many others. If they enjoyed the old pattern of ordained ministry, there may be a real sense of loss for its demise. This might be a process of bereavement that is as real as any other. The cleric will need to be a fairly secure person in order to respond positively to all these challenges. There will be the need to train and equip others for their work on top of a working week that continues to be busy. Others will need to be encouraged and supported in their developing pastoral ministries as they do more than the church will ever have asked them to do before. All of this will take place against the background of expressions of loss by some members of the church and the community for the demise of the old and much cherished way of doing things. This will sometimes be detected behind questions like, "But why isn't he/she going to be doing this?" The unspoken follow up is almost always that any decent minister would still be doing what the present one no longer does. That hurts but can never be allowed to anchor the church in ways that are resistant to the prompting of the Spirit. Determined resistance to change can't be allowed to provide our template for ministry in a changing world now and for the future.

New skills will need to be learned by everyone; for example, when to let things continue as people make mistakes and when to step in to sort something out. That's a judgment to make, a tough call we don't always get right. If "stepping in" is required for some reason, it is vitally important that the minister steps back out again. People need space to grow and develop in ministry; the cleric needs to honor that.

When the church embraces new patterns of ministry, busyness continues, but this is a genuinely productive busyness as the whole body of Christ works together. The minister will certainly make his or her own mistakes too. There aren't any blueprints or simple answers to difficult questions. All that can ever be hoped for is a wisdom that very slowly comes with experience.

Martyn will have continued to meet regularly with the wardens through all of this, in order to monitor things. At these sessions, much valuable ground will have been covered, many problems shared, much coffee drunk. How fortunate we can be as Anglicans/Episcopalians to experiment with new ways of being church as we draw on the wisdom and godly advice of wardens who remain available and active and, of course, continue to pray with and for the minister. In the parish here, over many years, we will have been blessed by churchwardens of considerable ability. It isn't an exaggeration to say that without them none of the good things the parish experienced would have taken place.

All of this embodies the very scriptural emphasis on the way we stand together in the life of the church. The Apostle Paul often uses the term "one another"; for example, the call to honor one another that is found in Romans 12:10. 1 John 3:18 mentions the importance of divine love within the church being expressed in practical ways. The battle for good and healthy expressions of living together in Christ is often won or lost in the arena of our relationships. There are no shortcuts!

The Spouse in the House

The need for change comes calling at the vicarage or rectory too. It isn't only the one who is formally ordained who is called to practice new patterns in the life of the church. When we are married to the person who is ordained, we are called to model new patterns of ministry too.

Many of us have an image of what we think a traditional clergy wife is or at least should be. She dresses conservatively, usually in a twin set with plain, long skirts and flat, sensible, lace-up shoes. Her only piece of jewelry will be pearls to offset her hair, which is always tied in a bun. She never rushes or gets uptight, despite endless work in the parish and vicarage. She cooks and bakes to perfection; answers the door and telephone with a cheerful air; makes endless cups of tea for meetings and visitors; keeps the vicarage and garden spotless, regardless of their size. The minister's clothes and vestments are always spotless and wrinkle-free. Her large family appears well behaved each Sunday morning, sitting silently in the front pew, and not even baby utters a whimper. In her spare time, she cleans the church, arranges the flowers; runs all women's work in the parish; serves on the PTA; does all the paperwork, including the parish magazine. She has given up her own career in order to serve the parish and manages effortlessly on an income half that of most of the parishioners.

Thankfully, that image is no longer one we recognize in our parishes. Many clergy spouses are now male, not female. Many choose to work full-time, some part-time; only a few choose not to work at all outside of the parish. The "buy one get one free" offer is now, rightly, something of a rarity. Of our many clergy friends, we find the wives/husbands are a massively diverse bunch. Each now chooses their own level of involvement in the parish and its life.

It is, however, the case that most clergy spouses have a living and real faith and would, therefore, choose to be actively involved in church life whomever they were married to. All of us live in clergy houses very much at the center of parish life so have to be involved in the taking of telephone messages and the answering of the door. Fay recalls with horror at twenty-two years old, being told by our first church that she was not expected to work, as she needed to stay at home to run the women's work. She replied that she needed to work to buy furniture, as at the time we had none. Something of the rebel, she was then told she had to stand on the church door to shake hands with everyone as they left, as this was her "job." She replied that her job was podiatry.

However, this proved invaluable in ministry, as Fay always tried to find out what God wanted her to do in each of the very diverse churches in which we served, rather than being committed to a set role based on the expectations of others, for which she may not have been called or gifted. It must be said, Fay has always been active and quite central in church life over the years, largely because we see ministry very much as a joint venture. Needless to say, her role has changed and evolved over the years.

One of the many blessings the parish of Cilybebyll gave us from the start was allowing Fay to be herself. This was quite a rare and welcome gift. A very few people clearly missed the old pattern for the rector and his wife—on occasions referred to, decades ago, as "the rector and the director." The vast majority realized these static models of ministry were past their "sell by" date and didn't fully allow people to exercise the ministries for which they were particularly gifted.

When we arrived in the parish in 1997, our children were quite small, so they demanded much time and attention. Fay found her role, therefore, to be more home-based .We held a lot of meetings at the rectory and invited people to tea or to pop in for coffee. She tried to alternate between the two churches in order to meet the whole parish. The parish youth group met at the rectory, where pizza cooking took place. Fay, being something of a geek, began doing much of Martyn's typing and e-mailing. Now she maintains the parish website, does the monthly notice sheet, and generally functions as his PA.

During the discernment process in the parish, many people had suggested that Fay should be included on the MDT. When the new structures were set up, she became the coordinator for the small groups team. She also serves as a worship leader.

Fay's ministry has therefore developed and changed

as the parish has changed and embraced more ministry on the part of parishioners, the baptized. However, it was appropriate that any change to her role and ministry will have been her response to the gifting that she and others will have discerned in her. Ministry undertaken solely at the behest of husband or parishioners would hardly have been fruitful!

Whoever we are, we can only honor God if we are led by him in the light of the different talents he will have given. There can never be a right or wrong model of ministry for the spouse in the house! We live and minister as the people we were created to be by God. After all, the pearls would never have looked quite right on a devotee of Meatloaf.

The Whole Congregation

During the life of our first set of new structures, the MDT and Caroline, the diocesan officer who was helping us, felt it was important to make our new structures "official" from the diocesan point of view. After all, the journey we had been taking as a parish was something the diocese had been encouraging; the Archbishop had also been actively involved in advising us as a parish. Our assistant bishop, Bishop David, came and blessed the work that was taking place here in a special service.

Much planning and preparation took place for this time of worship, which was to be for the whole parish and was held on a Sunday evening. Caroline had a number of possible orders of service from other dioceses; it was good to be able to draw on these as we planned our own.

Bishop David joined the MDT and their partners for tea at the rectory before the service began. The church was full, and there was a buzz of excitement about the whole thing. As people came in, they were given bookmarks with a simple order of daily prayer on them, plus a card with a prayer of commitment to God. We wished to emphasize that we were all involved in what we were doing as a parish; we were all being given an opportunity to recommit ourselves to God.

We had deliberately planned the service to reflect the usually diverse nature of our worship styles, so we had an organ with traditional hymns for part and the worship band accompanying some worship songs for other parts. Drama was included alongside liturgy. Many people were actively involved.

The bishop preached on 1 Corinthians 12 and reminded us that the Holy Spirit gives each of us gifts to use for the building up of the body of Christ.

As part of the act of worship, we all had an opportunity to stand and make promises to God and to be blessed by Bishop David. Members of each coordinating team stood, as did those who were on the MDT, the worship leaders' group, the church council, and the whole congregation. We were all involved in this, underlining that we are all part of the ministry and mission of the church into which we had been baptized.

This was to be an important evening for us all, not least to have official recognition by the diocese and its blessing. For the few people who weren't really convinced about these new structures, it was important that they saw the diocese "owning" them; the new patterns of ministry weren't simply a parish initiative or a mad idea from the rector. It was also helpful to make a public commitment or recommitment to God and his work, for he honors us when we honor him.

The bookmark pattern of daily prayer, produced by the Church in Wales, proved to be important for us too. We found that giving people a simple pattern like this to use in their daily devotions led to an increased desire for more resources on the part of many members of the church. We, therefore, wrote a slightly more lengthy pattern of daily prayer for those who find liturgical prayer helpful. These were made freely available in both of our churches. Around this time, we started providing Bible reading notes across the parish too, and many still find these very helpful in their daily devotional life.

This time of recommitment continues to encourage people as they grow in their faith and develop their spiritual life day by day. This, of course, is positive in itself and has a spin-off effect in the life of the parish and beyond.

Disappointments and Encouragements

Nothing is easy. Certainly moving from one understanding and practice of being the church to another is far from easy. In our weaker moments, it would have been a great comfort to have had a blueprint giving details of the end product, with easy-to-follow steps to get us there. Life isn't like that—church life definitely isn't.

Prayer had been a great source of encouragement to us along this road. When we didn't know what to do next, we still knew God and could pray about our frustrations and anxieties. God might not have given us a blueprint; what we were given instead was a sense that God could help us discover the next step and would give us enough faith to take it. From the beginning, we were convinced in prayer that God had asked us to trust him and that he would whisper "turn left" or "turn right" at the appropriate time. This meant that we would need to trust him every step of the way.

When we think we have a blueprint, we can easily end up not seeing the need to trust God at all.

It would be misleading to give the impression that everything we tried worked and that everyone in the parish loved the course on which we had embarked. It wasn't like that at all! We certainly had to learn that God doesn't undertake to bless our good ideas, the things we've decided to do for him. God will bless his ideas rather than ours! There were many things we tried over the years with an absolute confidence that the new initiative, whatever it was, would surely work; the need was there, the planning was there, the people were there to get things done, and it still didn't work! Coping with such disappointment is part of the journey of faith on which we had set out.

Not everyone was "on board" with the parish's new patterns of ministry either. It would be naïve to assume that as long as things are communicated with clarity everyone will be. There will always be those who, for whatever reason, remain wedded to the old pattern and can't see the need for any change at all. When any organization changes, however sensitively this is done, there will always be some who will step back and won't feel able to be actively involved as they once were. Of course, this is sad, but we must allow people freedom to choose. It remains of vital importance that they are not allowed to stop the unfolding of the story itself. God's people have always been on a pilgrimage, and it is so important to continue to walk with God into the future that he has planned for us.

We had decided as a church council that all of these new structures were going to have a life of three years. That was understood before we put the new structures in place. It was important that this understanding was part of the fabric of our new MDT and coordinating teams from the beginning; otherwise, we could easily have run the risk of setting up static, mini empires and giving jobs for life to those who might have been appointed to certain roles.

Though numbers didn't double in the parish over this period—in fact, numbers held steady rather than grew—the truth was that we had our encouragements too. These would have been encouragements that we could not have seen without having taken the road we had. We had taken on an aging congregation, and many fell away due to illness or perhaps moving to be near other family members. We had to add new people even in order to keep numbers static. New people were added, and some of these will have been in the thirties and forties age group that we lacked before. This helped us to look more like God's family, with a spread of ages, preferences, and talents.

All of this seemed to be in line with a conviction that had emerged as we had prayed over the years. We had been given a sense that God was putting "machinery" into the parish's life that would be needed later on. One of the prayer pictures colleagues had given us was of Noah's Ark being built and needing to have certain facilities and structures on board. This was our experience in practice.

It was interesting how many "words and pictures" were given to parishioners and people outside the parish as they prayed for us. We were hugely encouraged that so many of the people who shared words of encouragement with us were not card-carrying charismatics. They were simply God's people at prayer. They were those who were prepared to spend time in silence before God. During this whole period, in fact, a silent prayer group, "Listening to God," was set up and had been a massive encouragement to us. This fortnightly prayer group continues today. We can never know how many of the good things that were happening among us took place because God's people prayed. But waiting on God in prayer was an integral part of the life of the parish as we slowly moved forward.

How grateful we were to God that even though we had our share of disappointments, the things that encouraged us were far more numerous! God is gracious and knows how to encourage his children. As Psalm 1 underlines, when we attempt to model our life on the teaching God gives, rather than on anything else, we know what renewal, refreshment, and fruitfulness are.

Three Years Already!

I t didn't seem long before the MDT realized that its three-year life and that of the groups was coming to an end. The time had gone by very quickly. We now had some more serious thinking, praying, and planning to do.

The current MDT had to decide what to recommend to the church council for the way ahead. The MDT started to discuss which of our coordinating groups should change in some way or, perhaps, cease to exist. We needed to ask ourselves a number of questions as well. Were there any new groups or areas we felt God now wanted us to create? How could we best recommend to the church council that some of our current groups should continue? How could we handle the whole issue of the ministries of a number of us changing or developing? We would also need to be sensitive about how we handled some people standing down from their various roles during this first three-year period.

Much soul searching and discussion needed to take place in all these areas if we were to continue to encourage good and helpful practice in the life of the church. One recommendation we made to the church council at this stage was that three years was too short a life for an MDT and the coordinating groups. We felt we had just started carrying out some of the things we believed God wanted us to do when we were having to hand things on to those who would serve following the second discernment process that would soon be upon us. That said, we were aware that some of our people were becoming tired too. For this reason, we recommended that the next MDT should exist for a four-year period rather than for five years or more. We tried to look at each coordinating team in turn. We needed to listen to the views of the various members of the teams, not just to those of the coordinators. As a result of this period of reflection and review, a particular snapshot of the parish emerged.

The church beyond the church team had begun many good things and in many ways had begun the work of a pastoral, visiting group within the parish. It was quite natural, therefore, that we should recommend to the church council that it "morph" into a group with a more direct pastoral aim.

The small groups team felt that they had begun to do two separate jobs but couldn't really do both properly at the same time. The team suggested that perhaps the best thing would be for our cell groups and their teaching function to continue alongside a separate evangelism team.

We agreed that children's and youth work should continue to be a priority for us as a parish, as should the welcoming of young families into the life of church. We also knew that this area alone could occupy all of our efforts, resources, and time if we allowed it to. In this area in particular, we wanted to be realistic about recommending that we should attempt to do a few things well rather than burn people out in the frantic scrabble to do too much.

The building project in Alltwen was moving forward well and covering lots of good ground. We would almost certainly need a group to go on supervising the massive amount of work all of this entailed.

We were open to the need to consider new things in the parish as well. A number of possible areas for new work came to the surface as we chatted and prayed, one being the setting up of a world mission coordinating team. This might be able to help us to pull together and develop the work that was already taking place in this area in church.

Worship was discussed at length, partly as Martyn was feeling frustrated by how he alone was responsible to develop and move forward our diverse styles of worship. We discussed how we could best use the excellent worship leaders who were now in place. After much discussion, we recommended to the church council that worship development became a separate, new team, which was represented on the MDT but was, in many ways, a separate, distinct group functioning alongside it. It was exciting to see ministry developing among us as new groups and teams emerged out of the existing ones, almost like new petals forming out of the existing ones. This was a great encouragement to us, as it had been for this reason that the new structures had been set up in the first place.

We also chatted about other parishes and dioceses and their new patterns of ministry. We had so many ideas and possible recommendations for the way ahead. Somehow, we would need to narrow these down into something practical that we could sustain.

The MDT eventually handed over to the church council a large sheet of flip chart paper—where would we be without our flip charts?—containing many ideas and suggestions for the church council to think and pray about as it start planning and discussing the way ahead.

Moving Forward

When the church council met to begin to make decisions about our second pattern of ministry, it did so with a blank sheet of paper; teams might cease to exist, divide, or continue, but nothing was taken to have been penciled in as the church council started to consider the way ahead.

As we mentioned, the outgoing MDT had made tentative suggestions to the church council about a possible way forward. Some of the coordinating teams had made suggestions on the same basis as well. Throughout all of this, we had underlined that the church council and the minister had the final legal responsibility, together with the wardens; it would be as Anglicans/Episcopalians with Anglican/Episcopalian insights that our embracing of new patterns of ministry would take place.

We had a number of sessions as a church council in order to decide upon the areas of ministry in which our new structures would need to be active. It seemed appropriate that, although Martyn chaired the meetings as a whole, these extended discussions would be handled by a member of the church council with particular abilities in this area. We began by reviewing how things had gone over the past three years. As we did this in the light of our mission statement, we began to have a clearer picture of our priorities for the future. These outlined areas of ministry for our new coordinating teams for the next four years. It was still not easy to sift through so many good ideas and, instead, seek what God wanted us to do.

The areas upon which we finally decided were worship development, pastoral care, world mission, evangelism, and growing younger as a church. As before, the coordinators of each of these teams would serve on the MDT and help us, as a parish, move forward in making our mission statement something of a reality in our life together. We would need to make decisions and plan in these areas; good things couldn't happen by accident. We needed to identify people who could serve in line with the gifts God had given and others had recognized in them.

In order to begin to make these decisions, we needed another discernment service. We held this on the first Sunday in September 2006 in our parish church in Cilybebyll. The context for this was worship. As part of our time together, a member of the church council had guided our thinking together to help us prepare for the next four years. As we had done three years before, two sheets of paper were given to each person present (see Appendix 1 and 2). Again, we underlined that this was not a vote; we weren't going to have winners and losers. People were asked prayerfully to make notes of those whose names came to mind when we thought about each area of ministry. After this, we made notes about the particular qualities and abilities that came to mind when we thought about people we knew in church life—those we knew well and others we were getting to know.

The next step was for Martyn to meet with Caroline at a conference they both attended in order to collate the information and reflect about what God might be saying. As had been the case three years earlier when we had done this before, a clear picture emerged for the way ahead.

Certainly, this wasn't an example of a process being used in order to invite people to serve in line with what had already been privately decided. In fact, there were a number of areas of ministry in which we couldn't imagine who might be the right person to approach in order to coordinate work for us. After the collating and reflecting had been done by Martyn and Caroline, there was a sense of general agreement about what God was asking us to do together. It is always exciting to see where God leads, as, often, it is in the most unexpected ways.

We decided that we would need to introduce a worship development team (WDT) alongside the MDT. As areas of responsibility would overlap, it was decided that a member of the WDT would attend MDT meetings. They would attend on a rota basis, with a different WDT member attending each time. Martyn would serve on both groups as parish minister. We didn't know it then, but during the four-year life of these groups, we would be asking far-reaching questions about our worship patterns in the parish. This would not have been possible without the church council, MDT, and

WDT working very closely together without even the vaguest hint of turf wars.

As before, people were approached and invited to serve on the MDT for the next four years. An indication was given to each one about the area of ministry in which the church had thought it appropriate for them to be involved. The new MDT met for the first time for worship and discussion. At this meeting, we chatted about those who might be invited to serve on the various coordinating teams in the light of the discernment service held a couple of weeks earlier. For the second time, we were in a position to move forward with new structures in place and with people serving together in the light of their gifts and abilities. Again, we had no blueprint for the future; better than that, we had God, who would walk with us and guide us step by step. The next four years would be crucial in many ways, and there was a tangible sense of excitement among us.

A passage of Scripture that had been particularly important to us as a parish was Jeremiah 29:10–14. It is part of a letter written to God's people in exile in a distant land as they started to realize that they might be there longer than they would have wished. What sustained them was the sense that God was assuring them about all of the good things he had prepared for them in the future. They didn't know exactly what life would look like when they would eventually move back to their ancestral home in Judea. That God was encouraging them and reassuring them was enough. It was for us too.

Some Groups Continued

As we tentatively felt our way forward, it seemed to us that the reasons for establishing fellowship in a small group setting still held; fellowship in the context of cell groups should continue to be part of our life in the future. We had decided that some areas of ministry would need to continue into the next stage of the church's life, even if the brief of some of these would need to change slightly.

One of them, the growing younger coordinating team was, in effect, an extension of our earlier youth and preteens work. As a parish, we needed to emphasize to those who worked in this area that it was important for them only to attempt to do a few things well; they would need to work across the life of the whole parish, coordinating their work with those who worked in other areas of ministry as well. How easy it would have been for this team especially to attempt too much and burn itself out in the process. The original aim was for it not simply to look at youth and children's work in the life of the parish but also to look at ways we could become more family-oriented and welcome parents and their children into the life of church. We needed to grow younger as a church.

As is the case in so many churches, many of our young people continued to vanish during term time as they attended university in other parts of the country. This group, therefore, was aware of the need to welcome them back into the life of the parish during vacation time and often arranged various social events for them.

This team represents young families, teens, and preteens at the MDT; at MDT meetings, the group's coordinator was well placed to remind all of us to plan with these age groups in mind. The presence of this team's coordinator—a person with much experience in working with children—on the MDT was so useful in helping us all think about the decisions we were making concerning our new St. John's in Alltwen, even in simple things like making sure baby-changing facilities would be available. In addition, this team has been able to work with the WDT in planning family services and other worship events. By this stage in the life of the parish, it seemed quite natural to minister and make decisions in and through our new structures. The value of these continuing to work well was felt throughout the life of our churches.

We came to the conclusion that it was vitally important to have the needs of younger people represented in other aspects of the parish's life so that, in all of our activity and planning, they are borne in mind.

The church beyond the church team developed naturally into the pastoral care coordinating team. The minister's role needed to change in the light of all of this if he was to find time to help develop the ministries of us all in the parish. We decided, therefore, to set up a team of dedicated laypeople who could take communion to the housebound. We also felt it was important that these older members of church were still visited by the minister when possible but no longer on a regular monthly basis as before. The vast majority of our older people were more than happy with this arrangement and understood the reasoning behind the decisions we had made. The team often fed back problems and pastoral needs to the minister so the best possible care could be decided upon and offered to our elderly members.

Our evangelism team initially took over the development of the new church, as this building would be so important in every area of our life together, especially in our ability to reach out into the community for the sake of the gospel. They made sure that tools for future evangelism would be available in our new building. For example, they saw the need to install a café where many informal meetings, worship services, and evangelistic events could take place in a more relaxed setting. This room was to have a DVD player that would open up all sorts of exciting possibilities for evangelism, worship, and teaching. The main church area was equipped with a projector and a laptop so that PowerPoint could be used for the teaching ministry of the church.

A few months before we were due to open our new building, this team moved all of these discussions forward in earnest. An open day would take place, when appropriate, around the time the building was open in order to show members of the wider community the new facilities. What an important opportunity this would give us to invite people into our worshiping life.

The idea was that we would soon be welcoming members of the community into the church café for our first Alpha course in the new building. In this way, and in many others, we could see God's kindness at work in blessing us and giving us all that we needed to do what he was asking of us; there was a real sense of excitement in the life of the parish. These were clearly days that helped shape our life as we moved into the future hand in hand with the One who had good things in store for us.

World Mission

Over the years, various groups in the life of the parish had forged links with charities and mission organizations and attempted to support their work. Truth to tell, only those who belonged to the different parish organizations had any idea that all of this was taking place. The church council came to the conclusion that the church as a whole needed to be made more aware of the things we were already doing in this area, and so one of our new coordinating teams was asked to help us in the field of world mission. At first, its job was to simply make us all more aware of the things that were already taking place among us. The church council had tasked this group with moving us in whatever direction it thought best. There was the possibility of substantially reshaping our engagement with the world in this way, perhaps channeling our efforts into a single project if this seemed a useful way forward.

The world mission team realized that different groups in the parish were already heavily involved in various projects throughout the world. The team tried, from the start, to give this a sense of cohesion in order to ensure that we were not all trying to pull in different directions.

In addition to all of this, 10 percent of all the income that the parish receives is given to a number of charities. These charities are chosen by the church council with the intention of having a balance between local and worldwide work. Our present pattern is that five charities are chosen for two years. Then the exercise is repeated, and another five are selected. The reason for this approach is the desire of the church council not to set up anything that's given permanent status, thereby limiting what we could do in the future. It would be so easy to end up with a particular approach to engaging with the needs of the world that could never be changed in times to come. How easy it is for the Christian church to lose the sense that God is asking us to move on.

The team initially decided to put a list on our notice boards so that everyone would become more aware of what we were already supporting as a parish. Amongst the things supported early on, in this way, were Christian Solidarity Worldwide, a children's charity in Uganda, and the Welsh Air Ambulance scheme. There were many others.

This coordinating team also listed the various charities that our different groups helped. We have two ladies' meetings, and a Mothers' Union branch, all of which support charities by fundraising, giving out information for prayer and discussion, and often making direct contact with those helped. The parish organizations also welcome speakers who give updates about the work of our chosen charities.

Added to this, most church members have a number of charity boxes, for example, for the Archbishop of Wales Children's Fund, which replaced the Children's Society work here in Wales. At harvest time, people donate dried food, mostly pasta, which is taken to Romania by another local group. At Christmas, people are invited to fill a shoebox with Christmas gifts for children in poor communities. The world mission team was able to help us focus more effectively on all of this. Part of its task was to feed information to us so that our prayers for them would be better informed.

The church council had earlier discussed at length some of the dangers that can come to the surface when we attempt to engage with various needs in other parts of the world. One of the dangers is that of linking our humanitarian work with a particular political analysis of the situation. We had identified the significant danger of the parish adopting a series of political positions on the back of our desire to help people elsewhere. How easy it would be to exclude people, intentionally or unintentionally, if their understanding of the political situation differed from that of the minister and others on the church council.

We were determined from the start that we would not try to present simple political solutions to the world's complex problems; there wouldn't be a parish policy on global economics, for example. However, the church council was convinced that having a commitment to the God of all truth meant that we should never present partial and incomplete pictures of political issues; under no circumstances should we try to micromanage parishioners' political views or consumer choices. Our intention, instead, would be to fully celebrate our diversity as Anglicans/Episcopalians. We do this quite naturally in other areas of our life, and we were determined that it wouldn't be any different when it came to political views. Our different political understandings and commitments would be celebrated too; they were not a problem to solve. The church council, therefore, agreed that we would try to run this area of our life together without implying that if people held views that were different from our own, theirs were obviously lacking either in respect of morality or understanding. We would attempt to model an approach that embraced a commitment to treat those with whom we disagreed with courtesy and respect, even when it comes to politics.

It has always been the case that when people truly know and love God, they cannot fail but to be moved by the suffering of others. God seems to put different things on different people's hearts and minds, things in which he wants them to take a special interest. We have friends who have a massive commitment to people in New Zealand, others for Finland or Israel or those in Gaza and the West Bank. One of our friends helped to open orphanages in Uganda. Some are particularly committed to helping those with AIDS-related problems. It seems that God fires up his people with his passion and compassion for people in so many different ways. He is the One who sends people out to serve him when their hearts in some way overlap with his.

We wanted to get involved in all of this, perhaps in a small way at first. Throughout it all, our particular commitment as a parish continued to be with helping people come to Christ and grow in their love and knowledge of him. Caring for people's various needs and sharing the good news of the gospel with them are not mutually exclusive, after all!

Worship Development

We decided that because worship was so central to what we are as church it needed its own structure to monitor and develop each of the different styles across the parish. We wanted to make sure we offered God our best in worship, while making sure that individuals had an opportunity to develop and use their God-given ministries. Scripture says so much to us about worship. It's quite natural for us, as part of God's creation, to worship our Creator. It isn't an exaggeration to argue that we reach a level of complete fulfillment in life only when we give our worship of God its proper place.

The minister isn't always going to have enough time to develop each approach to worship to the extent it deserves. We, therefore, appointed four people to coordinate and develop each of our four worship streams in the parish, later adding a fifth. This group would meet together as a worship development team, with different members of it taking turns in attending the MDT group. Each had a small team of worship leaders on whom they could call to plan, lead, and assist with services.

Worship on Sunday mornings at our Norman country parish church uses modern language liturgy, but, overall, the character of it still feels particularly traditional. The coordinator of this worship stream developed the involvement of the congregation in the services. As many as wished could take part in a variety of ways. A different person each week helps lead much of the service alongside Martyn, with him as minister preaching the sermon and leading the prayer of thanksgiving and other various prayers at our Eucharists. Other people help with the readings, the psalm, and the prayers of intercession. In addition to all of this, others again help distribute communion to the congregation. It was so exciting to see people who initially had not been keen even to read a lesson now helping in ways that they would never have thought possible before.

Sunday mornings at our other, more modern, church had a very different feel to it again. Though it was still recognizably Anglican, it had more of the character of family worship, as the Sunday school is based there. All of this also involved lots of different people taking part in many ways. Once a month, we held a family service for people of all ages. This is informal in style, often with many taking part in dramas or helping to read material that would be easily understood in an "all-age" context. The inclusion of PowerPoint in the new church will help us develop this further.

At 5:30 p.m. on Sundays and on Wednesday mornings, we have reintroduced more traditional services using the Anglican *Book of Common Prayer*. This is greatly loved by many of the older people, who find they meet God in a special way through language with which they grew up; in many respects, the worship of this stream is considerably enhanced through the beauty and poetic nature of the language. This is another example of us trying to give of our best to God, who gives of his best to us. So much in these services is based on Scripture and wonderfully echoes the language of the authorized King James Version of the Bible.

On other Sunday afternoons, during most months, we have a modern language service in Welsh for our members for whom Welsh is their first language. Sometimes, material is used to help people reflect on their faith, and a mixture of modern and more traditional hymns is used. We have produced a simple-to-use order of evening prayer in a booklet for use on these occasions.

At 6:30 p.m. on Sundays, we have had informal worship for a number of years. This is intended for those who prefer the more charismatic style of worship, teaching, and prayer ministry as they celebrate their faith together. Guitar and keyboard accompany the leading of worship. Many different people lead this service in many different ways. On some occasions at the "6:30," the teaching follows a particular series. Many of us have found this a safe training ground as we have practiced the leading of worship. How good it is to be able to build others up and encourage them as we all celebrate our ministries.

There are times when those who usually attend the 5:30 and 6:30 services meet in between the services for fellowship and tea and coffee—something we all value. On special occasions, we will share a light tea of cakes or scones together (how very British!). We have been aware of the need to deepen friendships between those who attend our various worship streams.

On Wednesday evenings, we continue to meet together for worship, teaching, and the sharing of our faith in discussion groups. Sometimes, this takes place in church; at other times, we meet as three cell groups in homes. When we meet in church, we continue with our established pattern of church nights, with group discussion over tea and coffee continuing to be highly prized by all. It becomes increasingly natural for us to share our faith and views with others on these occasions and at cell groups in homes. Two of these meet on various afternoons; the other takes place on a Wednesday evening. Each group uses booklets we have produced containing the same study material, and this helps to develop the teaching life of the parish. If we hope to develop our ministries, this can only happen as there is development in our understandings of the Christian faith.

It is difficult to exaggerate the importance of the diverse styles of worship we use, as these help to allow a wide variety people's preferences to be held together side by side in the same parish. None of this would be possible without the empowering of all the people of God as we grow in our ministries and in our sharing together in Christ.

Bucking the Trend

As we have mentioned, much of the church in the West has been in decline for a number of years, including sections of it in the US. It has been against this background that many churches have developed new patterns of ministry. Opponents of new patterns of ministry argue that we need full-time, paid, professional ministers in each local church if the church is to move back into growth.

Much of the ministry that takes place in many Christian denominations is done either by those who are ordained or by those who are employed because they have a certain, trained ability. The second group includes people with particular skills in administration, those with expertise in youth work, education or music ministry. All of this is positive. It would be difficult to imagine the Church without them. The truth is still, however, that even at the beginning of the 21st Century, it is the minority of Church members who are active, and the majority passive.

Interestingly, over these same decades, a religion has established itself as something of a world religion built, principally, on the opposite approach when it comes to professional ministry. The religion in question is Mormonism, the Church of Jesus Christ of Latter-day Saints, and its growth has been nothing short of staggering, and all of this with full-time, professional ministers nowhere to be seen at local level.

The differences of theological understanding between the LDS church and those of traditional, historic Christianity are well known and well rehearsed. This certainly isn't the place to revisit them. What is interesting here is the growth of Mormonism at the local, "ward" level. In the Mormon ward, the saints are led by a bishop, a man who sustains himself financially with full-time, paid work elsewhere. The same is said of all of the church's local officials.

If we were to visit the Mormon church in our area, what we would find would be a high level of involvement from a significant number of people. There would be the ministry of teenagers (boys) in the Sunday sacrament service and the freedom of men, women, and children to play a full part in the teaching life of the church. The expectation of faithful Mormons is to be actively involved in the life of their church. The picture that emerges is of an energized people with a real sense of belonging to the ward. These structures are repeated throughout the LDS church around the world at local level, and everyone is aware that success and growth are only possible with the wholehearted involvement of everyone.

In this setting, the shared commitment to the gospel, as Mormons understand it, helps to generate a closeness of fellowship and belonging. It is out of this that high levels of involvement and activity are sustained. Not only are families and individuals journeying together, they also have a shared understanding about what the destination beyond death looks like. Added to this is a shared understanding of what a faithful Mormon life looks like in this world. We are in a world that desperately needs answers; for us, as Christians, we believe that Jesus is the answer that people need. If we were to imagine that clarity of belief is undesirable or surplus to requirements in our churches, we would miss the mark; we would fail to energize the very people that journey with us. We would, no doubt, face further decades of watching other world religions growing whilst we continue to decline.

With an energized people, like the Mormon people at local level, money is released to produce teaching and mission resources of staggeringly high standard, this by full-time, paid staff. The reading of the LDS scriptures, the local teaching of the Mormon faith, and the priority given to investing in mission become hallmarks of a confident religion that expects to encounter even better days in the future.

As the church's understanding of ministry develops, the battle against decline will, no doubt, be won or lost as we engage seriously with the importance of mission and the teaching of the faith. It's all of us, as God's people, that need to take this seriously. We can't simply load this on to the shoulders of one paid individual. We are all called to be involved in taking the sharing of our faith and Christian teaching seriously.

On Reflection

When we arrived in the parish, one of the hymns at the Induction was "All for Jesus, all for Jesus, this our song shall ever be, for we have no hope or Savior, if we have not hope in thee." We chose this because our prayer was that Jesus would be at the center of all we did, and everything we did would be for him and his glory. The final verse of this hymn sums up so much for us too: "All for Jesus, all for Jesus, this the church's song shall be." The older we both get, the more convinced we become that it is all about Jesus. Only in him do we find our true meaning and purpose. As individuals, we were created to worship God, and, therefore, when we come together as the church of Christ, worshipping him must be central in all we do. The emphasis can never be about what I get, like, or want, but what I can give to God alongside others.

It is said that one in six American Christians now change church every year! Almost certainly in the UK, we have set out along that road as well, as we so often seek that which demands the least and gives the most.

Perhaps it's fair to say that some of the negative characteristics of consumerism have molded and shaped us as Christians. It's so easy to think that Church is, somehow, there just to satisfy us. The danger is that we forget that we go to Church to worship God, and this ought to be expressed in the way we serve others and bear their needs in mind. It is difficult to imagine that spiritual maturity lies in a more self centered direction.

The Christian life, when healthy, really has to be about God rather that about me and my preferences. We are so grateful to God that our experience here in Cilybebyll has been about loyalty to Christ on the part of his people. There has been a sense of us increasingly valuing the part we are called to play in the body of Christ. It has been as we have tried to practice positive relationships with our brothers and sisters in Christ that all sorts of good and positive things have become possible. Of course, relationships are never easy; they often need hard work and a great deal of prayer, yet it is together with others that we slowly understand who we are called to be and develop the ministries the Lord has given us.

How grateful we are to have been called to minister here alongside others who have been prepared to think prayerfully about the way ahead. We have certainly had times of difficulty, but these have been massively outweighed by all of the good and positive things God has done among us. Throughout this period, it has been a privilege to have been called to be with others who know and love Christ and take the Bible seriously.

We have come to realize that, in these changing times in the church of Christ, the development of spirituality remains crucial. Together, we have an increasing sense of the awesome privilege we have of being coals aglow alongside others in the Spirit of God. How grateful we are to God for all that he has given us, together with his grace and mercy.

In changing times, he is the One who remains changeless; when security in other things increasingly breaks down, he is our rock and our protector. With him, there is always the sense that the best is yet to be.

Our new Church and café opened in the Summer of 2009. We are all excited about the new possibilities and challenges that lie before us. How good it is to know that God will continue to stir the fire of his Spirit among us as we look to him.

Epilogue

On July 5th 2009, I went to Alltwen to dedicate what had been a rather dilapidated church hall as the new church and community centre for the parish of Cilybebyll in Alltwen. As this book points out, the old church had become financially unviable, structurally unsound and the approach to it difficult to negotiate even for relatively fit people. The transformation of the existing hall into a multi-purpose building is a parable and symbol of the transformation that has happened in the parish as a whole over the last eleven years. New life has emerged from the old, on the foundations of all that had gone on before. For just as the structure of the old church hall forms the basis of the new centre, the new life of, and in the parish, has been built on the witness of previous generations of Christians.

Many parishes could learn from the example of Cilybebyll. There is always a temptation in believing that things will not work in our parish in the way they have in Cilybebyll because our parish is different, more difficult, or has not got the same resources. In fact, of course, what is needed is the gift of faith and the willingness to take risks which is what this parish did. When it set out to look at the way it worshipped, stewarded its resources, ministered to young people, used its buildings and tried to take the ministry of all the baptized seriously, it had no real idea of how things would work out or the direction the parish would take.

Led by the rector, the people of God set out like Abraham, not quite knowing where God would lead them but determined to trust in his care and providence. Everything the parish undertook was under girded with prayer and the knowledge that what it was doing was not attempting to become modern or successful, or reorganizing its own life, but seeking God's will for his mission and ministry in this particular community. All of that required openness to God and to new insights that the diocese was offering and a willingness at times, to get things wrong. This book tells the story of how it tried to do all that and my hope is that in reading the story of this particular church community, others will have the courage to pick up on some of the ideas and insights and be willing to do new things as well as old things in new ways. And the journey for Cilybebyll is not over because the journey is never over for any of God's people, for the God we believe in is "such a fast God, always before us, and leaving just as we arrive" as R. S. Thomas, the greatest priest poet of the twentieth century puts it.

The Most Rev Dr Barry Morgan. Archbishop of Wales.

Appendix 1

Teens: work with teenagers.				
Pre teens: how to develop our work with children and their families.				
Small groups: setting up small groups for study and fellowship.				
New building project: converting church hall into new church and hall with coffee bar.				
Church beyond the Church: caring for people in the community beyond the Church.				

Appendix 2

Name:
Characteristic:
Area of Minsitry:

Name:
Characteristic:
Area of Minsitry:

Name:

Characteristic:

Area of Minsitry:

Name:

Characteristic:

Area of Minsitry:

Appendix 3

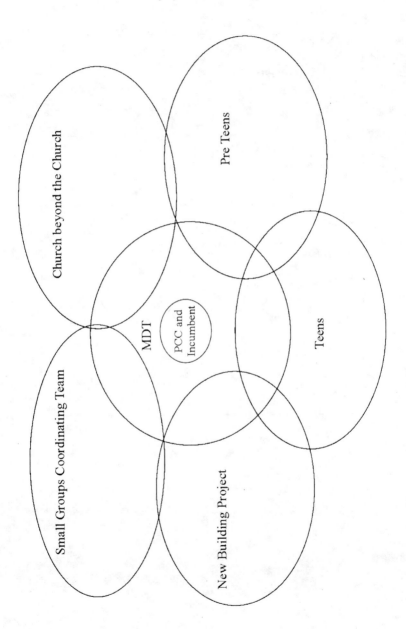

Church beyond the Church

Pre Teens

MDT

PCC and Incumbent

Teens

Small Groups Coordinating Team

New Building Project

Appendix 4

Guidelines for Parish Friends

What are Parish friends?

- Parish friends are parishioners who visit people who would appreciate extra friendship and an opportunity to chat. When the church launches a new ministry like this, it's often important to underline what this ministry isn't. Parish friends are not evangelists—that's a different ministry in the church. Neither are parish friends pastoral counselors or bereavement counselors. Again, these are different ministries.

- People are invited to become parish friends by the rector and the coordinator of the church beyond the church team following a decision at the ministry development team.

- A visit is embarked upon when a parish friend is asked by the rector and the church beyond the church coordinator. Members of the church beyond the church team help to oversee this ministry but are not parish friends themselves.

- During a "good" visit (the kind that the person being visited will appreciate) certain pieces of good practice are naturally used. When these tips are not used, problems can arise, and the effectiveness of the visit is greatly reduced.

Some Tips

- Make eye contact with the person being visited *from time to time*. This is an important skill to use.

- In a person's home, wait to be shown to a particular chair. To sit down uninvited in the chair of a recently deceased loved one, for example, can be unhelpful. Avoid sitting on a sofa or settee whenever possible. When people sit and face each other, as below (at "four o'clock"), this is best for occasional eye contact and a good visit.

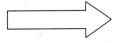

A good parish friend is there to listen, not to talk. Silences during a visit are not a problem unless these are awkward. Conversation can be restarted by feeding the final words spoken by the person back to them, e.g. "Your granddaughter has just started university?" or "Your son phoned yesterday?" This obviously is a technique, not an absolute and artificial rule, or the visit would turn into a type of radio comedy game.

- Never give advice on tricky problems and troubling issues—the church isn't there for that. If a problem or pastoral need arises, with the person's permission, privately speak to the rector.

- Never spend time during the visit assessing the interior décor of the person's home; this will be noticed!

- Never join in with gossip or the criticism of others. Visits must be discontinued if a person being visited insists on taking conversations in this direction.

- Dress modestly.

- If there is something a person being visited really wants to talk about, this might emerge on the third or fourth visit. Trust takes a long time to establish.

- Don't outstay your welcome—especially if the person is ill.

- Confidentiality is crucial. The person being visited is not to become material for a later conversation with someone else.

- Adopt a relaxed seated posture (but not horizontal and snoring). Don't fold arms or cross a leg.

- Don't yawn or look at your watch!

- It is always better not to visit a person on a regular basis, e.g. the second and fourth Thursdays of the month. It becomes harder to alter and reduce a pattern once it has been set in concrete. This opens the visitor up to the greeting, "And where were you last Thursday?"

- Don't overdo the visiting. Arrive at an amount that you can easily sustain without ignoring other important commitments you may have and the need to rest and generally to enjoy God.

- It is worth bearing in mind that there are always going to be some people who will only ever be satisfied with special treatment, which gives them much more attention than is offered to other needy people. In such circumstances, it is important to remember that "no" is not an unchristian word. To collude with selfishness on the part of a person making demands is neither good for the person concerned, nor for the parish friend. If a person tries to manipulate or bully a parish friend, the rector and the parish will always support the parish friend.

- It isn't good to take thirty minutes to leave a person's home.

- Don't expect to end every visit with solemn prayer. Prayer can be helpful between friends when trust has been established. Saying something along the lines of, "Would you like me to pray with you, or are you tired now?" gives them a get out clause if they are not comfortable with the idea. Pray a single, short prayer, and then only if both you and they are comfortable with the idea.

Don't Forget

- In being a parish friend, we have the privilege of being Jesus to the person we're visiting. The Holy Spirit makes us a blessing to the person.

- It is a good thing to pray for those we visit in our own home regularly. God can help and bless them ultimately much more than we can.

And Finally …

Thank you for being prepared to give your time and to share in this part of the church's ministry.

Appendix 5

Questions for Group Discussion
or Personal Reflection

1. Why is it important for God's people to "fire on all cylinders?"

2. What kind of talents and abilities does God give to his people?

3. Do we believe individually that we are able to use the gifts God has given us in our church life?

4. How can we end up thinking we have nothing to give to the ministry and mission of God's people?

5. What do we lack when we approach church life asking what we "get" from it?

6. What does God say to us when we feel that we're of little use?

7. Have you ever stepped out in faith and done something you didn't think you could do and then found God helped you to achieve it? Can you tell others your story to encourage them?

8. How can we discover our own gifts and abilities?

9. What opportunities does God give us to work alongside others in church life?

10. What kind of things can we learn from God over the years in our journey of faith?

11. How can we sometimes achieve more in life by doing less?

12. What are the characteristics of an unhealthy church?

13. What happens in church life when Christian leaders don't reflect the diversity we find amongst the people of God?

14. What examples of quarrelsome churches do we find in the letters of the Apostle Paul? Why did he take these problems so seriously?

15. How can having a good mission statement help us as a church?

16. What steps need to be taken to ensure that our forward planning has a practical edge?

17. What kinds of mistakes can a church make during times of change?

18. How can we help others feel that they "belong" in our fellowships?

19. How does our building affect the way we worship and live the Christian life together as a fellowship? What are our buildings' strengths and weaknesses?

20. How has the role of the minister/pastor changed over the years? Do we think the changes good or bad?

21. How can we encourage our pastor to minister in line with their actual gifts rather that the expectations of others?

22. How can we encourage others, even when their likes and dislikes, gifts and abilities are different from our own?

23. Why is it important for a church with big ideas to plan well and pray often?

24. What are the dangers of over planning for the future?

25. What particular things is God trying to impress upon the church these days?

26. Why is it important for the people of God to have a vision for the future and to work with God to bring it about in practice?

27. Why is it important that the creativity of the people of God can be expressed in our praise of God?

28. How can the church more effectively embrace the ministry of all God's people?

29. What practical steps can we take when we become aware that we are jealous of someone else's gift or ministry?

30. What positive response could we make to a person who argues that recent changes in church life are simply a matter of doing more, paying more and getting less?

Bibliography

Local Ministry. Story Process and Meaning, edited by Robin Greenwood and Caroline Pascoe. SPCK, London. 2006.

Total Forgiveness by R T Kendal. Hodder and Stoughton, London. 2003.

Contemporary Mormonism: Latter-day Saints in Modern America. Claudia L Bushman. Praeger. Westport, Connecticut. 2006.

Hope for the Church: Contemporary Strategies for Growth by Bob Jackson. Church House Publishing, London. 2006.

Today's New International Version. Zondervan. Michagan.2008.

Borgeson, Josephine and Lynne Wilson, eds. Reshaping Ministry: Essays in Memory of Wesley Frensdorff. Arvada, Colorado. Jethro Publications, 1990.

Original Intent by David Barton. WallBuilder Press, Aledo TX, 1996 and 2000.

The Book of Common Prayer. 1662.

listen|imagine|view|experience

AUDIO BOOK DOWNLOAD INCLUDED WITH THIS BOOK!

In your hands you hold a complete digital entertainment package. In addition to the paper version, you receive a free download of the audio version of this book. Simply use the code listed below when visiting our website. Once downloaded to your computer, you can listen to the book through your computer's speakers, burn it to an audio CD or save the file to your portable music device (such as Apple's popular iPod) and listen on the go!

How to get your free audio book digital download:

1. Visit www.tatepublishing.com and click on the e|LIVE logo on the home page.
2. Enter the following coupon code:
   1558-da7b-4e36-4325-1a58-701d-7e59-100c
3. Download the audio book from your e|LIVE digital locker and begin enjoying your new digital entertainment package today!